RAND McNALLY

Road Atlas

2016 MIDSIZE

CONTENTS

TRAVEL INFORMATION

Best of the Road® Trips ii-xii
Our editor's five favorite road trips from our Best of the Road® collection.

Tourism Contacts xiii
Phone numbers and websites for tourism information in each state and province.

Road Construction and Road Conditions Resources xiv-xv
Numbers to call and websites to visit for road information in each state and province.

Hotel Resources 81

Mileage Chart 82
Driving distances between 77 North American cities.

Mileage and Driving Times Map inside back cover
Distances and driving times between hundreds of North American cities and national parks.

MAPS

Map legend **inside front cover**

United States overview map **2-3**

U.S. states **4-53**

Canada overview map **54-55**

Canadian provinces **56-63**

Mexico overview map and Puerto Rico **64**

U.S. and Canadian cities **65-80**

Published and printed in U.S.A.

For licensing information and copyright permissions, contact us at permissions@randmcnally.com

If you have a comment, suggestion, or even a compliment, please visit us at randmcnally.com/contact
or write to:
Rand McNally Consumer Affairs
P.O. Box 7600
Chicago, Illinois 60680-9915

SUSTAINABLE FORESTRY INITIATIVE
Certified Sourcing
www.sfiprogram.org
SFI-00993
THIS LABEL APPLIES TO TEXT STOCK ONLY

Best of the Road® Trips

If you're like us, you love road trips. Here are some favorites from our Best of the Road collection. They follow scenic routes along stretches of coastline, both east and west; to forests, mountains, and prairies; and through small towns and big cities.

Boston

Massachusetts Maritime Tour

Fort Pickering Lighthouse, Salem

The close proximity to the Atlantic has long fostered a co-dependence between Massachusetts's coastal towns and the sea. To immerse yourself in the (aptly nicknamed) Bay State's rich maritime traditions, start at Newburyport's Custom House Maritime Museum on Boston's North Shore. Move from water to witches in Salem, home of the infamous trials.

A bit farther south, you'll hit the vibrant city of Boston, where history meets sports meets culture at every turn. Beyond, on the South Shore, you'll find Plymouth, famous landing place of the Pilgrims, and the Plimoth Plantation Living History Museum, where you can experience 17th-century life. Sights in the one-time whaling center of New Bedford highlight still more maritime history.

Distance: 135 miles point to point.

Type of Trip: Weekend Getaway; Arts & Music, History & Heritage, Picture Perfect.

Must Buy: Things that are very, very old. Antique stores abound in the town centers, and if you see signs for a yard sale or an off-the-beaten path antiques spot, be sure to stop. Families have been around for several generations, and lots of stuff gets handed down, whether it's wanted or not.

Newburyport

Custom House Maritime Museum. Settled in 1653 at the intersection of the Merrimack River and the Atlantic Ocean, Newburyport almost immediately solidified its importance as a commercial port. The museum, housed in a handsome Greek-revival building, contains objects that represent the town's maritime history. There are stunning models and paintings of the clipper ships that once plied their trade in this area as well as artifacts from actual ships that made it back to port and those salvaged from ships lost at sea. The museum's Coast Guard Room tells its history through art and photos and helps to explain exactly what the Coast Guard does. *25 Water St., (978) 462-8681, www.customhousemaritimemuseum.org.*

Salem

The Salem Witch Museum. Salem is most known for, of course, the 1692 Witch Trials, one of the strangest episodes in Anglo-American colonial history. Fourteen women and five men were hanged after being convicted of sorcery, and one man died after being pressed to death over the course of two days. The museum has stage-sets that use figures and narration to bring this frightening era to life. The gift shop sells all sorts of one-of-a-kind witchy paraphernalia including Salem witch bottles (small glass vessels filled with sand, salt, a nail, and a charm that colonists used to use to ward off evil). *Washington Sq., (978) 744-1692, www.salemwitchmuseum.com.*

Atlas map B-10, p. 11

Faneuil Hall

Boston

Faneuil Hall. Wealthy merchant Peter Faneuil built his namesake hall in 1741 to handle imported and exported goods (including, sadly, slaves). The building was used by Samuel Adams and other Sons of Liberty in the 1760s and '70s to denounce British Colonial rule. Still a popular venue for political speeches and public meetings, it now encompasses the original hall, as well as the North, South, and Quincy Market buildings. True to its commercial past, the whole complex is home to retail outlets, restaurants and bars, and small spaces that sell take-away food and souvenirs. *1 Faneuil Hall Sq., (617) 635-3105, www.cityofboston. gov/freedomtrail.*

New England Aquarium. Penguins, though not native to Boston, take pride of place here, but they're only a fraction of the aquarium's thousands of examples of marine life. Many different environments are recreated such as an Amazon rainforest, a coral reef, coastal Maine, and a harbor seal habitat. If you want to see whales—right whales, humpbacks, pilot whales—and dolphins, take the **Boston Harbor Cruises' New England Aquarium Whale Watch** (617/227-4321, www.bostonharborcruises.com/whale-watch), a three-hour tour offered in conjunction with the Aquarium. *1 Central Wharf, (617) 973-5200, www.neaq.org.*

Boston Tea Party Ships and Museum. On the evening of December 16, 1773, members of the underground group, Sons of Liberty, boarded three British trade ships anchored at Griffin's Wharf, and dumped their payload of tea chests into Boston Harbor. At this museum, you can board a replica of the *Beaver,* one of the ships at the wharf that night, and throw simulated bales of tea into the harbor. Abigail's Tea Room has tea (ahem), soft drinks, beer and wine, and assorted pastries and sandwiches. *Congress St. Bridge, (617) 338-1773, www.bostonteapartyship.com.*

Plymouth

Plimoth Plantation. This living-history museum recreates the daily life of Pilgrims and the native Wampanoags in 1627 through recreated homesteads, costumed re-enactors, and cooking demonstrations, lectures, and games. There's a crafts center, where workers use traditional tools and techniques to produce most of the items used on the grounds; a working grist mill; and the Nye Barn, where many of the animals are direct descendants of the cattle, sheep, goats, pigs, and birds the Pilgrims would have encountered or brought with them from England. The visitor center has a gift shop and a café. *137 Warren Ave., (508) 746-1622, www.plimoth.org.*

New Bedford

New Bedford Whaling National Historical Park. Whale-oil lamps were ubiquitous in the mid-19th century, and New Bedford was the world's premier whaling port and thus, the richest city. With a collection of museums, historic homes and buildings, and a working waterfront, the park invites you to explore the town in context of its golden past and its importance to the nation and the world. The visitors center has self-guided brochures and maps and a brief movie. Guided tours of New Bedford leave from the center daily and last about an hour. *33 William St., (508) 996-4095, www.nps.gov/nebe.*

Must See: Custom House Maritime Museum, Salem Witch Museum, Faneuil Hall, Boston Tea Party Ships and Museum, New England Aquarium, Plimoth Plantation.

Worth Noting: The best time to do this trip is the week right before Memorial Day (but not the weekend itself) because the weather is good yet the higher summer rates haven't yet kicked in (and won't do so till mid-June or after July 4th).

Early spring sees wildly unpredictable weather. Fall, on the other hand, offers that famous New England foliage. Winter is cold, but the holidays bring craft bazaars and Christmas-themed historic house tours.

Travel Tips: If you're flying, you can start at Boston's Logan International Airport or Providence's T. F. Green Airport, just 30 miles northwest of New Bedford, and then do this trip in reverse.

Plimoth Plantation

Heart of Indiana Tour

Eiteljorg Museum of American Indians and Western Art, Indianapolis

Distance: 97 miles point to point.

Type of Trip: Weekend Getaway; RV; Arts & Music, History & Heritage, Small Town Gems.

Must Buy: Creative types have flocked to Brown County for over a century. Crafts like weaving, leatherworking, and quilting are big. You'll also find unique jewelry, hand-painted silk scarves, and original works of art.

This tour samples the cultural vitality, scenic beauty, and increasingly sophisticated food scene in central Indiana. It begins in Indianapolis, the state capital, and then heads south to Columbus, one of the nation's top destinations for architecture lovers.

From Columbus, the road winds west into Brown County, a landscape of rolling ridges, mysterious hollows, and mist rising from forested valley floors. The American Impressionists of the Hoosier School migrated here to capture the countryside in watercolors and oils. Visit the T.C. Steele State Historic Site to hear their stories, or explore the wooded glens in Brown County State Park. A little farther west is Bloomington, a lively college town.

Indianapolis

Conner Prairie Interactive History Park. One of the nation's premier living-history museums brings 19th-century Indiana to life through costumed interpreters who go about their daily activities in five historic areas. Here you can be part of a Civil War raid, dance to a water drum and a gourd rattle in the Lenape Indian Camp, dip a candle at the William Conner Homestead, or learn about early aviation history at the 1859 Balloon Village. Note that the park is in the suburb of Fishers, about 25 miles northeast of downtown. *13400 Allisonville Rd., (317) 776-6006, www.connerprairie.org.*

Eiteljorg Museum of American Indians and Western Art. This museum celebrates the art, history, and cultures of North America's indigenous peoples and the American West. It has one of the nation's finest collections of contemporary Native American art as well as classic works by the likes of N.C. Wyeth, Frederic Remington, Charles Russell, and Kay WalkingStick. Its café serves Southwestern fare, and its store has many items produced by Native American artists. *500 W. Washington St., (317) 636-9378, www.eiteljorg.org.*

Atlas map F-4, p. 18

INDIANA

Edinburgh

Exit 76 Antique Mall. There's nothing fancy about this establishment, but treasures abound from more than 340 dealers displaying their wares in 600 booths and cases. Its 72,000 square feet make it one of the Midwest's largest antique malls. Those tired of shopping can relax in a lounge area with TV and vending machines. *12595 N. Executive Dr., (812) 526-7676, www.exit76antiques.com.*

Columbus

Columbus Architectural Tours. The Columbus Visitor Center offers a variety of tours of the city's internationally acclaimed architecture. Its signature two-hour guided bus excursion will introduce you to many of the nearly 70 eye-popping churches, commercial buildings, schools, and art installations. Along the way you'll learn about architects and artists that include I.M. Pei, Eliel Saarinen, Richard Meier, Harry Weese, Dale Chihuly, and Henry Moore. *506 5th St., (812) 378-2622, columbus.in.us.*

Gnaw Bone

Bear Wallow Distillery. This woman-owned business is continuing the long tradition of Hoosier moonshine, only with an upscale twist. Its copper stills create artisanal spirits from locally grown grains. Tours include samples of its signature liquors: Hidden Holler Corn Whisky Moonshine, Bear Trap Barrel Strength White Whiskey, and Liar's Bench Rye Whiskey. No need to worry about revenue agents—this moonshine is legal. *4484 E. Old State Rd. 46, (812) 657-4923, www.bearwallowdistillery.com.*

Nashville

Brown County State Park. Founded in 1929, this 16,000-acre oasis is nicknamed the Little Smokies because of its resemblance to the Great Smoky Mountains. Densely forested hills and valleys, rugged ridges, and deep ravines entice hikers and fall-foliage enthusiasts. *1450 State Rd. 46 E., (812) 988-6406, www.in.gov/dnr.*

T.C. Steele State Historic Site. Landscape painter Theodore C. Steele (1847–1926), the most highly respected of Indiana's painters, moved to Brown County in 1907 and helped introduce the area's beauty to an international audience. This state historic site preserves Steele's studio and home, which you can tour, as well as the gardens planted and tended by Selma Steele, the artist's wife. Five scenic hiking trails, from easy to steep, wind through the property, which also has a gift shop. *4220 T.C. Steele Rd., (812) 988-2785, www.tcsteele.org.*

Beanblossom

Bill Monroe Music Park & Campground. Known as the father of bluegrass music, Bill Monroe spent much of his life in tiny Beanblossom. His former home is now the site of the Bill Monroe Bluegrass Hall of Fame & Museum, featuring instruments, clothing, and memorabilia from the greats of bluegrass and country music collected during Monroe's 60 years as a performer. This is also where the world's oldest, continuous-running bluegrass festival is held: June's eight-day Bill Monroe Memorial Bluegrass Festival, which began in 1967 (make reservations well in advance). *5163 State Rd. 135 N., (812) 988-6422, www.billmonroemusicpark.com.*

Bloomington

Indiana University Art Museum. With a dramatically angled building designed by famed architect I.M. Pei and 40,000 objects dating from ancient Mesopotamia to the present, this is considered one of the country's top university art museums. There are paintings by Claude Monet, Jackson Pollack, and Pablo Picasso, and highly regarded collections of ancient jewelry and African masks and art. Angles Café—named after the building's unusual design—refreshes you with beverages and pastries. *1133 E. 7th St., (812) 855-5445, www.indiana.edu.*

Must See: Conner Prairie Interactive History Park, Eiteljorg Museum of American Indians and Western Art, Columbus Architectural Tours, T.C. Steele State Historic Site.

Worth Noting: Many restaurants here are locally owned and use locally sourced ingredients, guaranteeing a Midwestern-fresh meal. This is particularly true of Bloomington, where more than 100 one-of-a-kind eateries reflect not only the region's farm-to-fork philosophy but also the community's ethnic diversity.

Travel Tips: Plan your trip for the fall to take advantage of the brilliant foliage that will line much of the route outside of Indianapolis. Brown County is particularly scenic and sponsors a full slate of fall-themed festivals.

Brown County State Park

Columbus architecture

South Carolina: Highlights of Lowcountry

Marsh near Charleston

A road trip along coastal South Carolina means a relatively straight shot through seaside towns, many of which seem frozen in the elegance of a different era. From the 60-mile stretch of golden Grand Strand beaches to the mansions of historic Charleston to the plantations and seaside towns in between, Lowcountry charms you with its historical and natural beauty, great food, and Southern hospitality.

And, when you're not learning to dance the shag in North Myrtle Beach, you'll be touring centuries-old plantations and some of the country's oldest public gardens or following in the footsteps of movie stars in Beaufort, which served as the backdrop for classics like *Forrest Gump*.

Distance: 230 miles point to point.

Type of Trip: Weekend Getaway; RV; Arts & Music, Great Outdoors, History & Heritage, Picture Perfect.

Must Buy: A sweetgrass basket; these exquisite traditional creations are still hand-woven by members of the Gullah-Geechee communities all along the coasts of the Carolinas and Georgia.

Must See: Fat Harold's Beach Club, Myrtle Beach Boardwalk, Brookgreen Gardens, Fort Sumter National Monument, Middleton Place, Hunting Island State Park.

North Myrtle Beach

Atlas map F-8, p. 37

Fat Harold's Beach Club. You can't blend in with the locals until you can dance like them, and in Lowcountry that means learning the shag. This is one of the best places to get in step. The king of shag and founder of this club, Harold Bessent, wouldn't have it any other way. The Society of Stranders (SOS), a group devoted to the dance, holds events here, and the calendar is chockablock with lessons—some of them free. *212 Main St., (843) 249-5779, www.fatharolds.com.*

Myrtle Beach

Myrtle Beach Boardwalk and Promenade. The heart of Myrtle Beach is its boardwalk, which runs from a pier at 14th Avenue North to another at 2nd Avenue North. Take a spin on the SkyWheel, or fly above things on a Myrtle Beach Zipline Adventures experience. **Broadway at the Beach** (www.broadwayatthebeach.com) has over two dozen restaurants; several theaters; myriad specialty shops; and attractions like WonderWorks, Ripley's Aquarium, and the Hollywood Wax Museum. The Pavilion Nostalgia and Carousel Park has tamer vintage offerings. *14th Ave. N. to 2nd Ave. N., myrtlebeachdowntown.com.*

Murrells Inlet

Brookgreen Gardens. In 1931, four rice fields were transformed into public gardens that, today, often make top-10 lists of the nation's best. Themed landscape areas include Live Oak Allee, with trees planted as far back as the 18th century; a medieval-style labyrinth; and the Palmetto Garden, which features the Sabal palmetto, South Carolina's state tree. Kids love the zoo filled with Lowcountry creatures, the Enchanted Storybook Forest, and the Children's Discovery Room and Sensory and Nature Trail. *1931 Brookgreen Dr., (843) 235-6000, www.brookgreen.org.*

Charleston

Fort Sumter National Monument. There's an eerie calmness at Fort Sumter, the same place that was shaken by explosions that set the American Civil War in motion. In the early hours of April 12, 1861, the fort came under Confederate attack and surrendered 34 hours later. It was left a smoldering heap of ruins in Charleston Harbor. Over time, it was rebuilt and is now listed on the National Register of Historic Places, a testament to the resiliency of the American South. Vessels operated by **Fort Sumter Tours** (843/722-2628, fortsumtertours.com) depart several times daily from Liberty Square, near the Fort Sumter Visitor Education Center. Trips last just over two hours. *Liberty Square, 340 Concord St., (843) 883-3123, www.nps.gov/fosu.*

Middleton Place. The estate of Henry Middleton, President of the First Continental Congress, has decorative and fine arts from the mid-18th to the mid-19th centuries that document the history of this affluent South Carolina family. In addition to taking a 45-minute guided house tour, you can explore America's oldest formally designed garden, a vast landscape where there's something blooming just about year round: camellias in the winter; azaleas in the spring; magnolias, crepe myrtles, and roses in the summer. This National Historic Landmark site also has a restaurant serving plantation cuisine for lunch and dinner and an inn offering modern accommodations. *4300 Ashley River Rd., (843) 556-6020, www.middletonplace.org.*

Kiawah Island

Beachwalker Park. Just 15 miles south of Charleston, the barrier island's only public park consistently makes the *Forbes* list of America's best beaches. There are dressing areas and bathrooms, picnic areas with grills, and seasonal beach chair and umbrella rentals as well as showers. The beach is just one reason to visit the island. Golf is another. The island, much of which is a gated resort community, has five championship courses. *8 Beachwalker Dr., (843) 768-2395, www.ccprc.com.*

Beaufort

Beaufort Tours. Beaufort was voted America's Happiest Seaside Town, and this tour operator aims to show you why. See locations used in films like *Forrest Gump* and *Something to Talk About*. Explore a haunted graveyard on a ghost tour, or visit a cotton plantation on the Plantation and Gullah Tour. A two-hour walking tour of Beaufort's historic district is also available. *1006 Bay St., (843) 838-2746, www.beauforttoursllc.com.*

St. Helena Island

Hunting Island State Park. Along with miles of sandy beaches and a working lighthouse, this island has more than 5,000 acres waiting to be explored. White egrets, great blue herons, osprey, bald eagles, pelicans, loggerhead turtles, and alligators are some of the creatures that make their homes here. The park also has nature trails and a nature center, a fishing pier, a boat ramp, and a store. *2555 Sea Island Pkwy., (843) 838-2011, www.huntingisland.com.*

Charleston

Worth Noting: Charleston is home to many interesting annual festivals including Charleston Fashion Week (Mar.), Spring Festival of Houses and Gardens (mid-Mar.–mid-Apr.), and Spoleto Festival USA, celebrating performing arts (late May–early Jun.).

Travel Tips: If you're looking to enjoy the beach, June through August has the best weather and most activity. Spring and fall bring cheaper prices and cooler temperatures, but it's still possible to enjoy a beach vacation. If your focus is exploring Charleston, plan to visit between March and May or from September to November. Midsummer's high temperatures can interfere with a good time. Myrtle Beach is located an hour and a half from Wilmington, NC; 2 hours and 45 minutes from Columbia; and 3.5 hours from Augusta. Fly into any of these (Wilmington is the only international airport), or opt to fly into Charleston International.

Cannon at Fort Sumter

Texas Hill Country

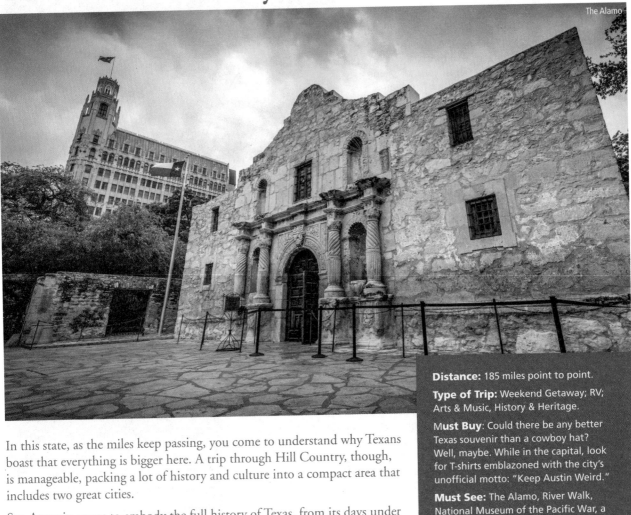

The Alamo

Distance: 185 miles point to point.

Type of Trip: Weekend Getaway; RV; Arts & Music, History & Heritage.

Must Buy: Could there be any better Texas souvenir than a cowboy hat? Well, maybe. While in the capital, look for T-shirts emblazoned with the city's unofficial motto: "Keep Austin Weird."

Must See: The Alamo, River Walk, National Museum of the Pacific War, a live show in Austin.

In this state, as the miles keep passing, you come to understand why Texans boast that everything is bigger here. A trip through Hill Country, though, is manageable, packing a lot of history and culture into a compact area that includes two great cities.

San Antonio seems to embody the full history of Texas, from its days under Spanish and Mexican rule to its struggle for independence ("Remember the Alamo," as the saying goes) and eventual statehood. Cutting-edge Austin, on the other hand, is the repository of all that history. Between them, you'll discover Wild West towns (some on the region's Wine Trail) that seem in no hurry to leave the 19th century.

San Antonio

The Alamo. In 1836, nearly 200 farmers, lawyers, surveyors, frontiersmen (including Jim Bowie and Davy Crockett), and others barricaded themselves inside the Alamo, determined to protect what they hoped would be the provisional capital of the Republic of Texas. Despite desperate requests for reinforcements, fewer than 100 men answered the call. Outside the walls, Mexico's Santa Anna marshaled his 1,800 men and waited. On March 6, the 13th day of the siege, Mexican soldiers breached the walls and killed all but a few women, children, and slaves, who were told to share what they had seen.

Atlas map F-8, p. 47

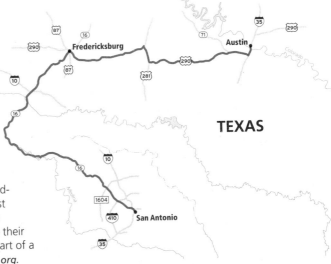

Hearing what happened on fact-filled ranger-led or self-guided-audio tours of the Alamo provides insight into one of the most unforgettable stories in American history. So does touring the museum within the Long Barrack, where the defenders made their final stand, and exploring the surrounding grounds, built as part of a WPA project. *300 Alamo Plaza, (210) 225-1391, www.thealamo.org.*

Field of Indian Paintbrush and Bluebonnets

River Walk. Designer Robert Hugman's vision of a lovely "scenescape" called Paseo del Rio, or River Walk, caught the imagination of San Antonio's citizens. It was completed as a WPA project, and to this day, its sinuous canals are enchanting, whether you walk along the promenade with its restaurants, cafés, bars, hotels, and boutiques, or embark with **San Antonio Cruises** (210/244-5700, www.riosanantonio.com) on a sail past scenes of old San Antonio. *110 Broadway, (210) 227-4262, www.thesanantonioriverwalk.com.*

Fredericksburg

National Museum of the Pacific War. Chester Nimitz grew up in land-locked Fredericksburg, but he went on to become one of the most respected of the U.S. Navy's admirals during WW II. This complex includes not only the Admiral Nimitz Museum but also the Center for Pacific War Studies, Plaza of Presidents, Memorial Courtyard, and Japanese Garden of Peace. Displays are packed with singular items like a PT boat, a Quonset hut, a mock field hospital, a midget Japanese sub that tried to reach Pearl Harbor, and the casing for a spare Fat Man atomic bomb. *340 E. Main St., (830) 997-8600, www.pacificwarmuseum.org.*

Dooley's 5-10-25. This place is a blast from the past, selling everything from broomstick toy ponies to Mexican jumping beans. What else can you stock up on? Things like Radio Flyer wagons, cast-iron cookware, kitchen gadgets, wind-up alarm clocks, plastic flowers, coonskin caps, Beemans gum, Blue Waltz perfume. . . the list goes on. *131 E. Main St., (830) 997-3458.*

Auslander. Combine a Bavarian biergarten with a Texas sports bar, and you get the Auslander. Drop into its bar or its German restaurant and select from roughly 70 beers, including those from Texas, Colorado, California, and Pennsylvania as well as those from Mexico, Holland, Belgium, Germany, and England. *323 E. Main St., (830) 997-7714, theauslander.com.*

Austin

Bullock Texas State History Museum. You can't miss this museum: Just look for the giant, bronze Lone Star sculpture. The first floor has Native American and Western artifacts, including an original wooden gate from the Alamo. Second-floor exhibits focus on the people and events that made Texas what it is—information you'll glean from diaries and letters dating from the days of early Mexican settlers, the Republic of Texas, the Civil War, and the Great Depression. The third level covers state geography, climate, infrastructure, and resources. *1800 N. Congress Ave., (512) 936-8746, www.thestoryoftexas.com.*

Waterloo Records. Music is the motor that moves Austin, and that motor is fueled by places like Waterloo Records. One of the city's finest record shops is packed with new and used CDs and LPs, including alternative/indie, rock/pop, folk/country, or blues/jazz. Texas artists are well represented, and the music-loving staffers will help you find new sounds. *600 N. Lamar Blvd., (512) 474-2500, www.waterloorecords.com.*

Congress Avenue Bridge Bat Colony. More than a million Mexican free-tail bats, comprising North America's largest urban colony, hang out beneath the Ann W. Richards Congress Avenue Bridge. Just after sunset, you can stand on its span, and watch the entire colony emerge for its nightly food foray. The viewing "season" runs March through November; late July or early August sees lots of young pups starting to fly. Want viewing-time information? Call the Bat Hotline, which is really just the main number for a local branch of Bat Conservation International. *(512) 327-9721.*

Worth Noting: This region is amid the heart of Texas wine country, where the **Wine Trail** (texaswinetrail.com) will take you on a vintage drive between Austin and Fredericksburg and New Braunfels. Also, consider timing your trip to experience a festival: South by Southwest (Mar.), Austin's premier music festival; Fiesta San Antonio (Apr.), whose roots go back to the 1890s; and Fredericksburg's Oktoberfest. When can you see the Texas state flower? Well, those bluebonnets are blooming best during the first two weeks of April.

Travel Tips: It can get supernaturally hot here in summer, with temperatures easily exceeding 90 degrees on most days—so plan accordingly. If you're heading into remote areas, pack some ice and water as well as snacks. Also, flash floods are common during heavy downpours; check weather reports before heading out and pay attention to signs indicating flood zones.

River Walk, San Antonio

A Pacific Northwest Passage

Cannon Beach

Distance: 442 miles point to point.

Type of Trip: Weekend or Vacation Getaway; RV; Arts & Culture, Great Outdoors, History & Heritage, Picture Perfect, Quirky & Oddball.

Must Buy: Jewelry or art created by any of the Pacific Northwest's Native American tribes; a wool Pendleton camp blanket or throw (think classic stripes or tartans in rich earthy or primary colors), woven in Oregon since 1863.

Woods, water, and historic wonders await on this trip between two great metropolises of the Pacific Northwest. Few cities balance culture and commerce, nature and architecture, the past and the future as well as Seattle. The Emerald City makes a great jumping off point for a visit to the Olympic National Park and Forest.

The coastal route south from forested Washington to Oregon is as fun to drive as it is breathtaking. It also promises unique maritime experiences in towns like Astoria and Cannon Beach. Inland, you'll travel through one of Oregon's wine regions before reaching Portland, the so-called City of Roses, known for its gardens and its greenery. Here, as elsewhere along the route, expect great food, great views, and great stories—old and new.

Seattle, WA

Pike Place Market. Founded in 1907, "the Market" is a multilevel complex overlooking Elliott Bay and part of a 9-acre historic district. At street level on its western side are produce, fish, meat, flower, and craft stands. Across the narrow, cobblestoned Pike Place are more shops and restaurants. Watch fishmongers toss salmon, visit the first Starbucks outpost, and enjoy the antics of talented street performers. *85 Pike St., (206) 682-7453, www.pikeplacemarket.org.*

Space Needle and Seattle Center. The 1962 Seattle World's Fair left a legacy of icons, including the 605-foot Space Needle and its 360-degree views. Glass elevators travel up to 10 mph to the observation deck, with its displays, shops, lounge, and revolving SkyCity restaurant.

Below the Space Needle are the Experience Music Project, with rock-and-roll memorabilia; the Pacific Science Center; and the Seattle Children's Museum. Arrive via the Monorail, which zips (in about 2 minutes!) between downtown's Westlake Center Station and Seattle Center Station. *400 Broad St., (206) 905-2100, www.spaceneedle.com.*

Atlas map C-4, p. 51

A Pacific Northwest Passage

Bill Speidel's Underground Tour. This 90-minute guided tour travels beneath historic Pioneer Square to 1890s walkways, where many storefronts and some interiors remain intact. You'll learn about Seattle's early timber days and famous Skid Row and get the back story of this three-block area, where the street level was raised from 8 to 35 feet after the 1889 Seattle Fire. *608 1st Ave., (206) 682-4646, www.undergroundtour.com.*

Port Angeles

Olympic National Park. Three ecosystems make up this 1,427-square-mile peninsular park: Pacific shoreline, subalpine forest and meadowland, and coastal-Northwest rain forest. You can readily combine a visit here with explorations of Olympic National Forest—which rings the park—and the coast.

The drive along U.S. 101 has many overlooks and short trails down to the beach. Near shore, in the park's southwestern reaches, is the Hoh Rain Forest. Learn about the mild climate and lush vegetation at its visitors center before exploring the mile-long Hall of Mosses or one of eight other trails. *3002 Mount Angeles Rd., (360) 565-3130, www.nps.gov/olym.*

Astoria, OR

Columbia River Maritime Museum. A massive window overlooks the Columbia River, and displays tell the stories of its vessels and the dangers they face on "the bar" at the river's mouth. Indeed, the collection of 30,000 maritime artifacts has many items salvaged from wrecks in the so-called Graveyard of the Pacific. Step into a simulator to see what it's like to pilot a tugboat before visiting the lightship *Columbia*. *1792 Marine Dr., (503) 325-2323, www.crmm.org.*

Cannon Beach

Ecola State Park. Kayakers and swimmers like the waters off this park's beautiful, half-mile Crescent and Indian beaches. You can also hike to a spot overlooking the 19th-century Tillamook Rock Lighthouse (in spring and fall, watch for gray whales). It's just off the 2.5-mile Clatsop Loop Trail, which travels through forests of giant Sitka spruce in the footsteps of Lewis and Clark. *Off Hwy. 101, (503) 436-2844, www.oregonstateparks.org.*

Forest Grove

David Hill Vineyards and Winery. Established by a German pioneer family in the late 1800s, David Hill has some of Willamette Valley's oldest Pinot Noir vines and also produces Gewürztraminer, Riesling, and other varieties. Stop by the tasting room any day of the week. *46350 N.W. David Hill Rd., (503) 992-8545, www.davidhillwinery.com.*

Portland

Pittock Mansion and Washington Park. Mansion is an understatement. It's more like a castle, or rather, a French Renaissance–style chateau. In the 1850s, Henry and Georgiana Pittock each traveled west along the Oregon Trail before meeting and marrying in Portland. Henry took over the *Daily Oregonian* newspaper and made a fortune in several endeavors.

Their 22-room sandstone residence was completed in 1914, and tours of it and the 46-acre estate highlight architecture, decorative arts, and the family. In nearby Washington Park, check out the Rose Test Garden, Japanese Garden, Discovery Museum, Portland Children's Museum, and Oregon Zoo. *3229 N.W. Pittock Dr., (508) 823-3623, pittockmansion.org.*

Powell's City of Books. It's been around for a while, is open 365 days a year, stocks new and used tomes, and has staffers and customers who truly love to read. Shop for books on local history or lore, scan the national best sellers, grab a cheap paperback, and have a cuppa at World Cup Coffee & Tea. *1005 W. Burnside, (503) 228-4651, www.powells.com.*

Must See: Pike Place Market, Space Needle, Hoh Rain Forest in Olympic National Park, Columbia River Maritime Museum, Pittock Mansion, Powell's City of Books.

Worth Noting: You can explore both Seattle and Portland below ground on tours of the Seattle Underground network of tunnels or excursions into Portland's Shanghai Tunnels. And, oh, if these passageways could talk. . . .

Travel Tips: To shorten the point to-point trip to 300 miles—without missing a thing—head south of Seattle through Olympia (the state capital and home to the national forest headquarters) to Aberdeen, down the coast, and inland to Portland.

To lengthen it into a full 625-mile loop, continue north from Portland through Washington State wine country (www.washingtonwine.org) in Vancouver, Longview, and Centralia before returning to Seattle via Olympia.

Hoh Rain Forest, Olympic National Park

Pittock Mansion, Portland

Tourism Contacts

On the road or before you go, log on to the official tourism website of your destination. These websites offer terrific ideas about organizing a visit and often include calendars of special events and activities. Prefer calling? Most states offer toll-free numbers.

United States

Alabama Bureau of Tourism & Travel
(800) 252-2262
(334) 242-4169
www.alabama.travel

State of Alaska Tourism Office
(800) 862-5275
www.travelalaska.com

Arizona Office of Tourism
(866) 275-5816
(602) 364-3700
www.arizonaguide.com

Arkansas Department of Parks & Tourism
(800) 628-8725
(501) 682-7777
www.arkansas.com

California Tourism
(877) 225-4367
(916) 444-4429
www.visitcalifornia.com

Colorado Tourism Office
(800) 265-6723
www.colorado.com

Connecticut Office of Tourism
(860) 256-2800
www.ctvisit.com

Delaware Tourism
(866) 284-7483
www.visitdelaware.com

Visit Florida
(888) 735-2872
(850) 488-5607
www.visitflorida.com

Georgia Department of Economic Development
(800) 847-4842
www.exploregeorgia.org

Hawaii Visitors & Convention Bureau
(800) 464-2924
(808) 923-1811
www.gohawaii.com

Idaho Tourism
(800) 847-4843
(208) 334-2470
www.visitidaho.org

Illinois Office of Tourism
(800) 226-6632
www.enjoyillinois.com

Indiana Office of Tourism Development
(800) 677-9800
www.visitindiana.com

Iowa Tourism Office
(888) 472-6035
www.traveliowa.com

Kansas Department of Wildlife, Parks & Tourism
(800) 252-6727
(785) 296-2009
www.travelks.com

Kentucky Department of Travel
(800) 225-8747
www.kentuckytourism.com

Louisiana Office of Tourism
(800) 994-8626
www.louisianatravel.com

Maine Office of Tourism
(888) 624-6345
www.visitmaine.com

Maryland Office of Tourism
(866) 639-3526
www.visitmaryland.org

Massachusetts Office of Travel & Tourism
(800) 227-6277
(617) 973-8500
www.massvacation.com

Travel Michigan
(800) 644-2489
(888) 784-7328
www.michigan.org

Explore Minnesota Tourism
(888) 868-7476
(651) 296-5029
(651) 757-1845
www.exploreminnesota.com

Visit Mississippi
(866) 733-6477
(601) 359-3297
www.visitmississippi.org

Missouri Division of Tourism
(573) 751-4133
(800) 519-2100
www.visitmo.com

Montana Office of Tourism
(800) 847-4868
www.visitmt.com

Nebraska Tourism Commission
(888) 444-1867
(877) 632-7275
www.visitnebraska.com

Nevada Commission on Tourism
(800) 638-2328
(775) 687-4322
www.travelnevada.com

New Hampshire Division of Travel and Tourism Development
(603) 271-2665
(800) 386-4664
www.visitnh.com

New Jersey Division of Travel & Tourism
(609) 599-6540
www.visitnj.org

New Mexico Tourism Department
(505) 827-7400
www.newmexico.org

New York State Division of Tourism
(800) 225-5697
www.iloveny.com

North Carolina Division of Tourism
(800) 847-4862
(919) 733-4171
www.visitnc.com

North Dakota Tourism Division
(800) 435-5663
(701) 328-2525
www.ndtourism.com

TourismOhio
(800) 282-5393
www.discoverohio.com

Oklahoma Tourism & Recreation Department
(800) 652-6552
www.travelok.com

Travel Oregon
(800) 547-7842
www.traveloregon.com

Pennsylvania Tourism Office
(800) 847-4872
www.visitpa.com

Rhode Island Tourism Division
(401) 278-9100
(800) 556-2484
www.visitrhodeisland.com

South Carolina Department of Parks, Recreation & Tourism
(803) 734-1700
www.discoversouthcarolina.com

South Dakota Department of Tourism
(605) 773-3301
(800) 732-5682
www.travelsd.com

Tennessee Department of Tourist Development
(615) 741-2159
www.tnvacation.com

Texas Tourism
(800) 452-9292
www.traveltex.com

Utah Office of Tourism
(800) 200-1160
(801) 538-1900
www.utah.com

Vermont Department of Tourism and Marketing
(800) 837-6668
(800) 882-4386
www.vermontvacation.com

Virginia Tourism Corporation
(800) 847-4882
www.virginia.org

Washington Tourism Alliance
(800) 544-1800
www.experiencewa.com

Destination DC
(800) 422-8644
(202) 789-7000
www.washington.org

West Virginia Division of Tourism
(800) 225-5982
(304) 558-2200
www.wvtourism.com

Wisconsin Department of Tourism
(800) 432-8747
(608) 266-2161
www.travelwisconsin.com

Wyoming Office of Tourism
(800) 225-5996
(307) 777-7777
www.wyomingtourism.org

Canada

Travel Alberta
(800) 252-3782
www.travelalberta.com

Destination British Columbia
(604) 660-2861
www.hellobc.com

Travel Manitoba
(800) 665-0040
(204) 927-7838
www.travelmanitoba.com

Tourism New Brunswick
(800) 561-0123
www.tourismnewbrunswick.ca

Newfoundland & Labrador Tourism
(800) 563-6353
(709) 729-2830
www.newfoundlandlabrador.com

Northwest Territories Tourism
(800) 661-0788
www.spectacularnwt.com

Nova Scotia Tourism Agency
(800) 565-0000
(902) 424-5000
www.novascotia.com

Ontario Tourism Marketing Partnership Corporation
(800) 668-2746
www.ontariotravel.net

Prince Edward Island Tourism
(800) 463-4734
www.tourismpei.com

Tourisme Québec
(877) 266-5687
(514) 873-2015
www.bonjourquebec.com

Tourism Saskatchewan
(877) 237-2273
(306) 787-2300
www.sasktourism.com

Tourism Yukon
(800) 661-0494
www.travelyukon.com

Mexico

Mexico Tourism Board
(800) 446-3942
www.visitmexico.com/en

Puerto Rico

Tourism Company of Puerto Rico
(800) 866-7827
www.puertorico.com

Road Work

Road construction and road conditions resources

Road closed. Single lane traffic ahead. Detour.
When you are on the road, knowledge is power. Let Rand McNally help you avoid situations that can result in delays, or worse. Use the state and province websites and hotlines listed on this page for road construction and road conditions information.

United States

Alabama
(888) 588-2848
www.dot.state.al.us

Alaska
511
511.alaska.gov
www.dot.state.ak.us

Arizona
511
(888) 411-7623
www.az511.com
www.azdot.gov

Arkansas
(800) 245-1672
(501) 569-2374
(501) 569-2000
www.arkansashighways.com

California
(800) 427-7623
www.dot.ca.gov
Los Angeles/metro area:
511, www.go511.com
Sacramento Region:
511, www.sacregion511.org
San Diego area:
511, www.511sd.com
San Francisco Bay area:
511, www.511.org

Colorado
511
(303) 639-1111
(303) 573-7623
www.cotrip.org

Connecticut
(860) 594-2000
(860) 594-2650
www.ct.gov/dot

Delaware
(800) 652-5600
(302) 760-2080
www.deldot.gov

Florida
511
(866) 374-3368
www.fl511.com
www.dot.state.fl.us

Georgia
511
(888) 635-8287
(877) 694-2511
(404) 635-8000
www.511ga.org

Hawaii
(808) 587-2220
hidot/hawaii.gov

Idaho
511
(888) 432-7623
www.511.idaho.gov
www.itd.idaho.gov

Illinois
(800) 452-4368
(312) 368-4636
www.gettingaroundillinois.com
www.dot.il.gov

Indiana
(866) 849-1368
(317) 232-5533
www.in.gov/dot

Iowa
511
(800) 288-1047
www.511ia.org
www.iowadot.gov

Kansas
511
(866) 511-5368
(785) 296-3566
511.ksdot.org
www.ksdot.org

Kentucky
511
(866) 737-3767
www.511.ky.gov
transportation.ky.gov/

Louisiana
511
(877) 452-3683
www.511la.org
www.dotd.la.gov

Maine
511
(866) 282-7578
(207) 624-3595
www.511maine.gov
www.maine.gov/mdot

Maryland
511
(855) 466-9511
(410) 582-5650
www.md511.org
www.roads.maryland.gov

Massachusetts
511
Metro Boston: (617) 986-5511
Central: (508) 499-5511
Western: (413) 754-5511
www.mass511.com
www.mhd.state.ma.us

Michigan
(800) 381-8477
(517) 335-3084
www.michigan.gov/drive

Minnesota
511
In MN (800) 657-3774
(651) 296-3000
www.511mn.org
www.dot.state.mn.us

Mississippi
511
(601) 987-1211
(601) 359-7001
www.mdot.ms.gov
www.mdottraffic.com

Missouri
(888) 275-6636
(573) 751-2551
www.modot.org

Montana
511
(800) 226-7623
(406) 444-6200
www.mdt511.com
www.mdt.mt.gov

Nebraska
511
(800) 906-9069
(402) 471-4533
www.511.nebraska.gov
www.dor.state.ne.us

Nevada
511
(877) 687-6237
(775) 888-7000
www.nevadadot.com
www.nvroads.com

New Hampshire
511
(603) 271-6862
www.nhtmc.com
www.nh.gov/dot

New Jersey
511
(866) 511-6538
www.511nj.org
www.state.nj.us/transportation

New Mexico
511
(800) 432-4269
(505) 827-5100
www.nmroads.com
www.dot.state.nm.us

New York
511
(888) 465-1169
(518) 457-6195
www.511ny.org
www.dot.ny.gov
Thruway:
(800) 847-8929
www.thruway.ny.gov

North Carolina
511
(877) 511-4662
www.ncdot.gov
www.ncdot.gov/travel/511

North Dakota
511
(855) 637-6237
(866) 696-3511
www.dot.nd.gov
www.dot.nd.gov/travel-info-v2/

Ohio
(614) 466-7170
www.dot.state.oh.us
www.buckeyetraffic.org
Cincinnati/metro area:
511
Ohio Turnpike:
(440) 234-2030
(440) 234-2081
www.ohioturnpike.org

Oklahoma
(877) 403-7623
(405) 425-2385
www.okladot.state.ok.us

Oregon
511
(800) 977-6368
(503) 588-2941
www.oregon.gov/odot
www.tripcheck.com

Pennsylvania
511
(888) 783-6783
www.dot.state.pa.us

Rhode Island
511
(888) 401-4511
(401) 222-2450
www.dot.ri.gov/travel

South Carolina
511
(877) 511-4672
(855) 467-2368
www.dot.state.sc.us
www.511sc.org/

South Dakota
511
(866) 697-3511
www.sddot.com
safetravelusa.com/sd/

Tennessee
511
(877) 244-0065
www.tn511.com
www.tdot.state.tn.us

Texas
511
(800) 452-9292
(512) 463-8588
www.txdot.gov
www.drivetexas.org

Utah
511
(866) 511-8824
(801) 887-3700
www.udot.utah.gov
www.utahcommuterlink.com

Vermont
511
(800) 429-7623
www.511vt.com
www.aot.state.vt.us

Virginia
511
(800) 578-4111
(800) 367-7623
www.511virginia.org
www.virginiadot.org/travel

Washington
511
(800) 695-7623
www.wsdot.wa.gov/traffic

Washington, D.C.
311
(202) 737-4404
(202) 673-6813
www.ddot.dc.gov

West Virginia
511
(877) 982-7623
www.wv511.org
www.transportation.wv.gov

Wisconsin
511
(866) 511-9472
www.511wi.gov

Wyoming
511
(888) 996-7623
www.wyoroad.info

Canada

Alberta
(877) 262-4997
www.ama.ab.ca

British Columbia
(800) 550-4997
www.drivebc.ca

Manitoba
511
(877) 627-6237
(204) 945-3704
www.manitoba.ca/roadinfo
www.manitoba.ca

New Brunswick
511
(800) 561-4063
(506) 459-3939
www.gnb.ca/roads

Newfoundland & Labrador
Avalon Region (709) 729-2382
Eastern Region (709) 466-4120
Central Region (709) 292-4300
Western Region (709) 635-4127
Labrador Region (709) 896-7840
www.roads.gov.nl.ca

Nova Scotia
511
(888) 780-4440
(902) 424-3933
511.gov.ns.ca/map

Ontario
511
In ON: (800) 268-4686
In Toronto: (416) 235-4686
www.mto.gov.on.ca/english/
traveller/

Prince Edward Island
511
(902) 368-4770
In Canada: (855) 241-2680
www.gov.pe.ca/roadconditions

Québec
511
(888) 355-0511
In Québec: (877) 393-2363
www.quebec511.gouv.qc.ca/en/

Saskatchewan
(888) 335-7623
Saskatoon area: (306) 933-8333
Regina area: (306) 787-7623
www.highways.gov.sk.ca/
road-conditions

Mexico

www.sct.gob.mx/carreteras

Puerto Rico

www.dtop.gov.pr/carretera

Get the Info from the 511 hotline

The U.S. Federal Highway Administration has begun implementing a national system of highway and road conditions/construction information for travelers. Under the new plan, travelers can dial 511 and get up-to-date information on roads and highways.

Implementation of 511 is the responsibility of state and local agencies.

For more details,
visit: www.fhwa.dot.gov/trafficinfo/511.htm.

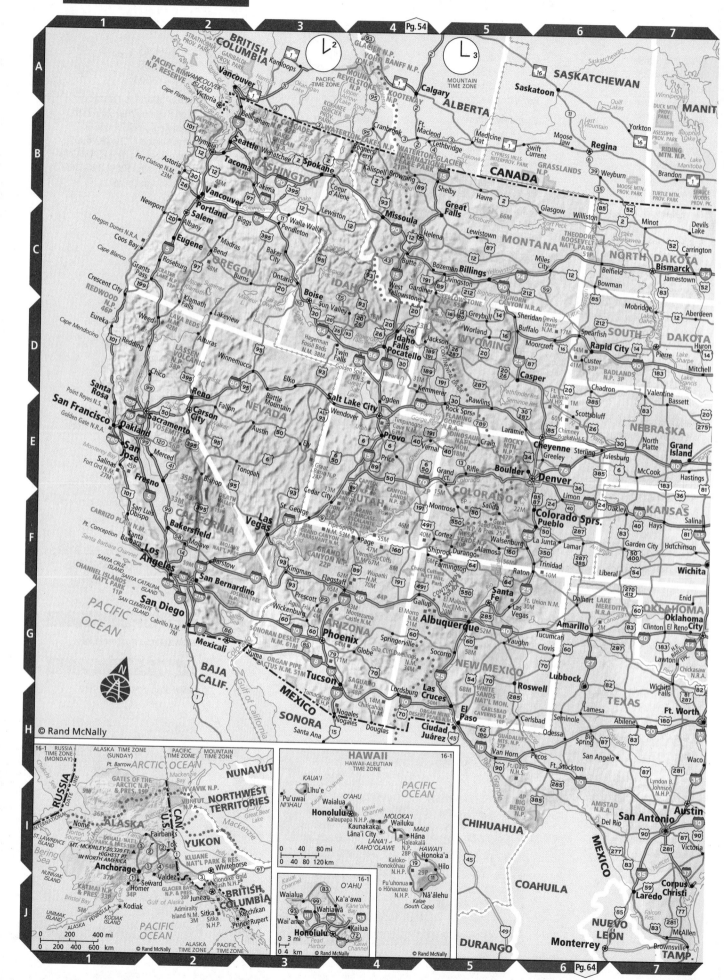

© Rand McNally

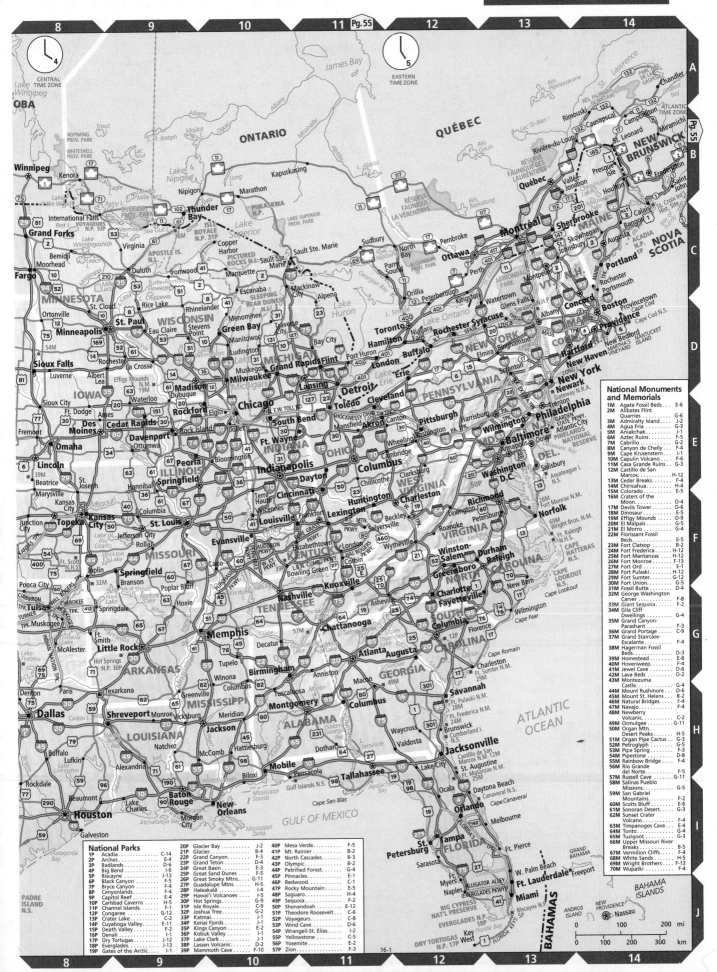

National Parks and National Monuments and Memorials map of the United States.

National Monuments and Memorials

1M Agate Fossil Beds ... E-6
2M Alibates Flint Quarries ... G-6
3M Admiralty Island ... J-2
4M Agua Fria ... G-3
5M Aniakchak ... J-1
6M Aztec Ruins ... F-5
7M Cabrillo ... G-2
8M Canyon de Chelly ... F-4
9M Cape Krusenstern ... I-1
10M Capulin Volcano ... F-6
11M Casa Grande Ruins ... G-3
12M Castillo de San Marcos ... H-12
13M Cedar Breaks ... F-4
14M Chiricahua ... H-4
15M Colorado ... E-5
16M Craters of the Moon ... D-4
17M Devils Tower ... D-6
18M Dinosaur ... E-5
19M Effigy Mounds ... D-9
20M El Malpais ... F-5
21M El Morro ... F-5
22M Florissant Fossil Beds ... E-5
23M Fort Clatsop ... B-2
24M Fort Frederica ... H-12
25M Fort Matanzas ... H-12
26M Fort Monroe ... F-13
27M Fort Ord ... E-1
28M Fort Pulaski ... H-12
29M Fort Sumter ... G-12
30M Fort Union ... D-5
31M Fossil Butte ... D-4
32M George Washington Carver ... F-8
33M Giant Sequoia ... F-2
34M Gila Cliff Dwellings ... G-4
35M Grand Canyon-Parashant ... F-3
36M Grand Portage ... C-9
37M Grand Staircase-Escalante ... F-4
38M Hagerman Fossil Beds ... D-3
39M Homestead ... E-8
40M Hovenweep ... F-4
41M Jewel Cave ... D-6
42M Lava Beds ... D-2
43M Montezuma Castle ... G-4
44M Mount Rushmore ... D-6
45M Mount St. Helens ... B-2
46M Natural Bridges ... F-4
47M Navajo ... F-4
48M Newberry Volcanic ... C-2
49M Ocmulgee ... G-11
50M Organ Mtn. Desert Peaks ... H-5
51M Organ Pipe Cactus ... G-3
52M Petroglyph ... G-5
53M Pipe Spring ... F-3
54M Pipestone ... D-8
55M Rainbow Bridge ... F-4
56M Rio Grande del Norte ... F-5
57M Russell Cave ... G-11
58M Salinas Pueblo Missions ... G-5
59M San Gabriel Mountains ... F-2
60M Scotts Bluff ... E-6
61M Sonoran Desert ... G-3
62M Sunset Crater Volcano ... F-4
63M Timpanogos Cave ... E-4
64M Tonto ... G-4
65M Tuzigoot ... G-4
66M Upper Missouri River Breaks ... B-5
67M Vermilion Cliffs ... F-4
68M White Sands ... H-5
69M Wright Brothers ... F-13
70M Wupatki ... F-4

National Parks
1P Acadia ... C-14
2P Arches ... E-4
3P Badlands ... D-6
4P Big Bend ... I-6
5P Biscayne ... J-13
6P Black Canyon ... F-5
7P Bryce Canyon ... F-4
8P Canyonlands ... F-4
9P Capitol Reef ... E-4
10P Carlsbad Caverns ... H-5
11P Channel Islands ... F-1
12P Congaree ... G-12
13P Crater Lake ... C-2
14P Cuyahoga Valley ... E-11
15P Death Valley ... F-2
16P Denali ... I-1
17P Dry Tortugas ... J-12
18P Everglades ... J-13
19P Gates of the Arctic ... I-1
20P Glacier Bay ... J-2
21P Glacier ... B-4
22P Grand Canyon ... F-3
23P Grand Teton ... D-4
24P Great Basin ... E-3
25P Great Sand Dunes ... F-5
26P Great Smoky Mtns. ... G-11
27P Guadalupe Mtns. ... H-5
28P Haleakala ... I-5
29P Hawai'i Volcanoes ... I-5
30P Hot Springs ... G-9
31P Isle Royale ... C-9
32P Joshua Tree ... G-2
33P Katmai ... J-1
34P Kenai Fjords ... J-1
35P Kings Canyon ... E-2
36P Kobuk Valley ... I-1
37P Lake Clark ... I-1
38P Lassen Volcanic ... D-2
39P Mammoth Cave ... F-10
40P Mesa Verde ... F-5
41P Mt. Rainier ... B-2
42P North Cascades ... B-3
43P Olympic ... B-2
44P Petrified Forest ... G-4
45P Pinnacles ... E-1
46P Redwood ... C-1
47P Rocky Mountain ... E-5
48P Saguaro ... H-4
49P Sequoia ... F-2
50P Shenandoah ... E-12
51P Theodore Roosevelt ... C-6
52P Voyageurs ... C-8
53P Wind Cave ... D-6
54P Wrangell-St. Elias ... I-2
55P Yellowstone ... C-5
56P Yosemite ... E-2
57P Zion ... F-3

Alabama

Population: 4,779,736
Land Area: 50,744 sq. mi.
Capital: Montgomery

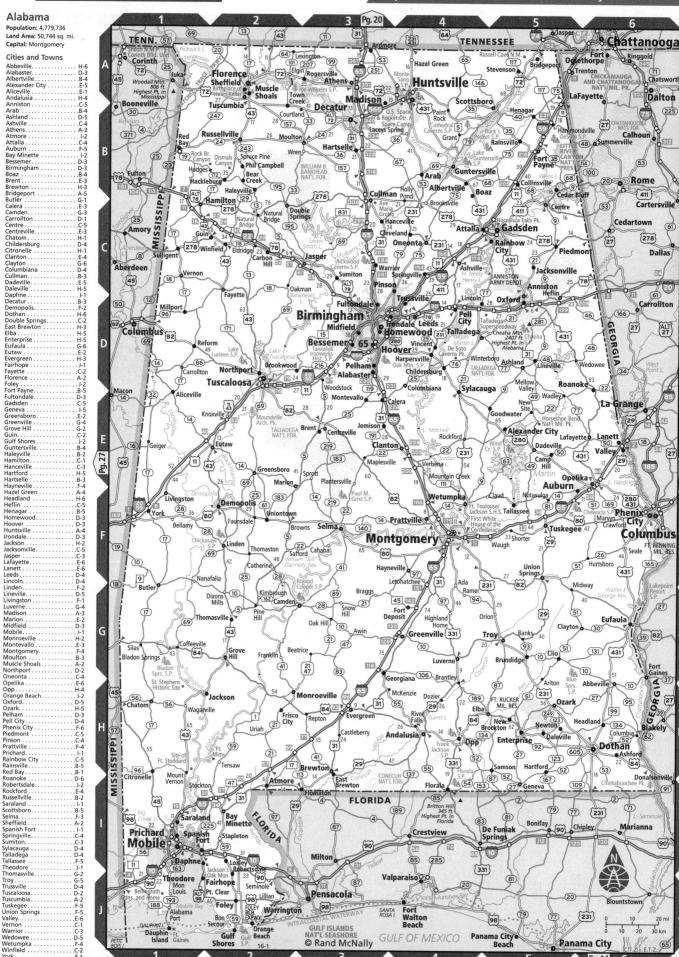

© Rand McNally

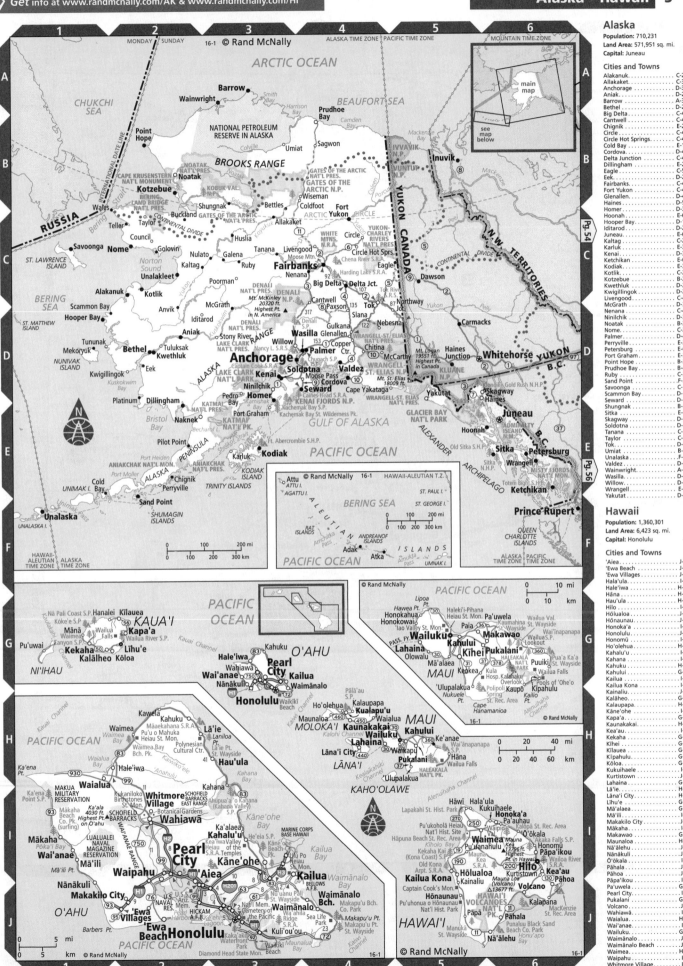

Alaska

Population: 710,231
Land Area: 571,951 sq. mi.
Capital: Juneau

Hawaii

Population: 1,360,301
Land Area: 6,423 sq. mi.
Capital: Honolulu

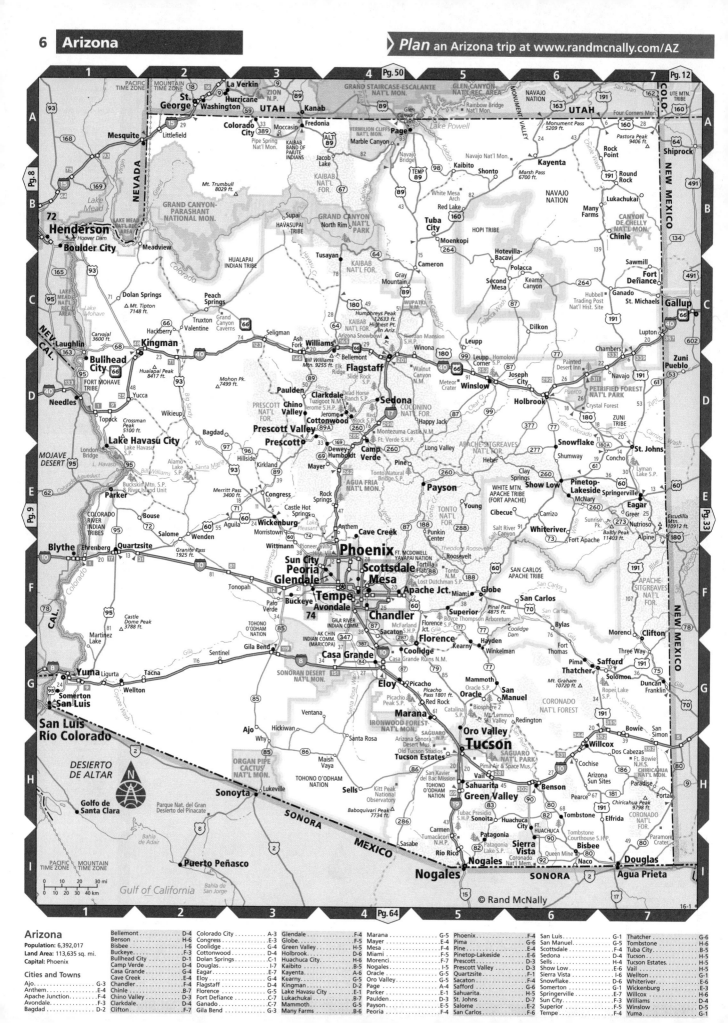

Arizona

Population: 6,392,017
Land Area: 113,635 sq. mi.
Capital: Phoenix

Cities and Towns

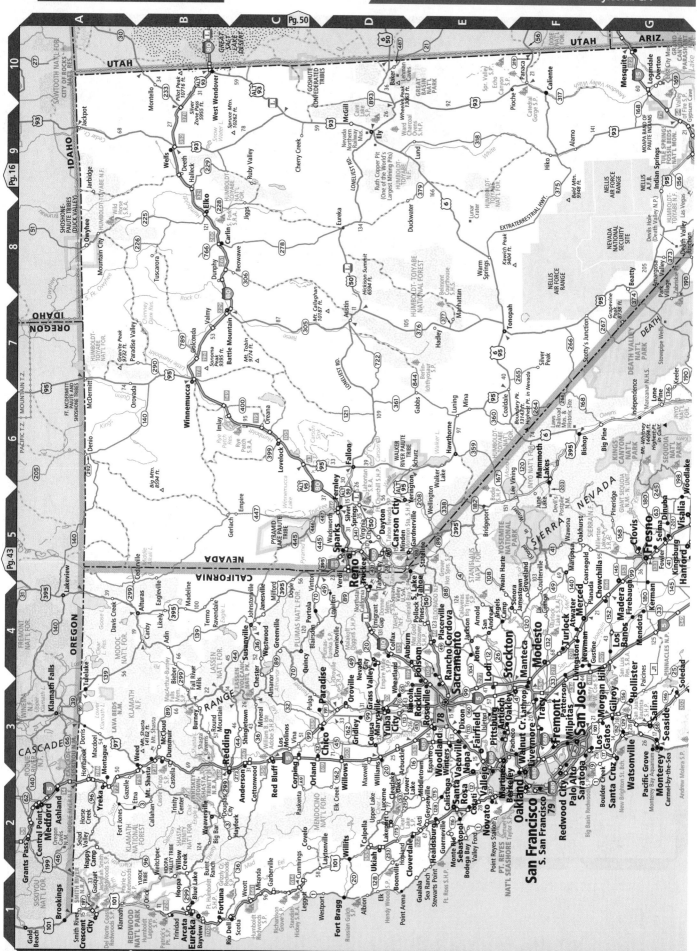

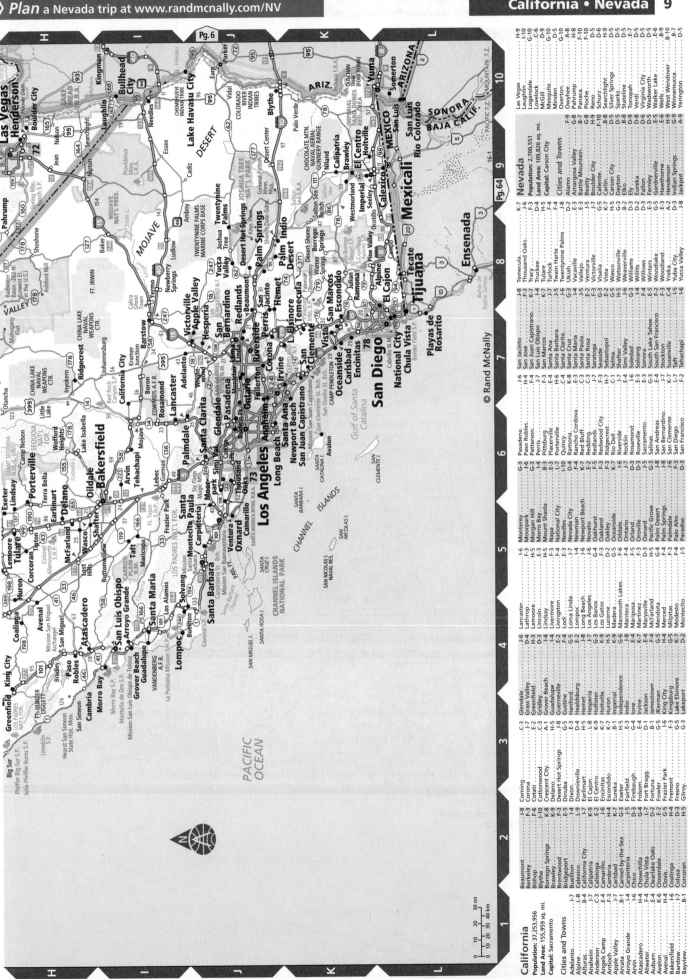

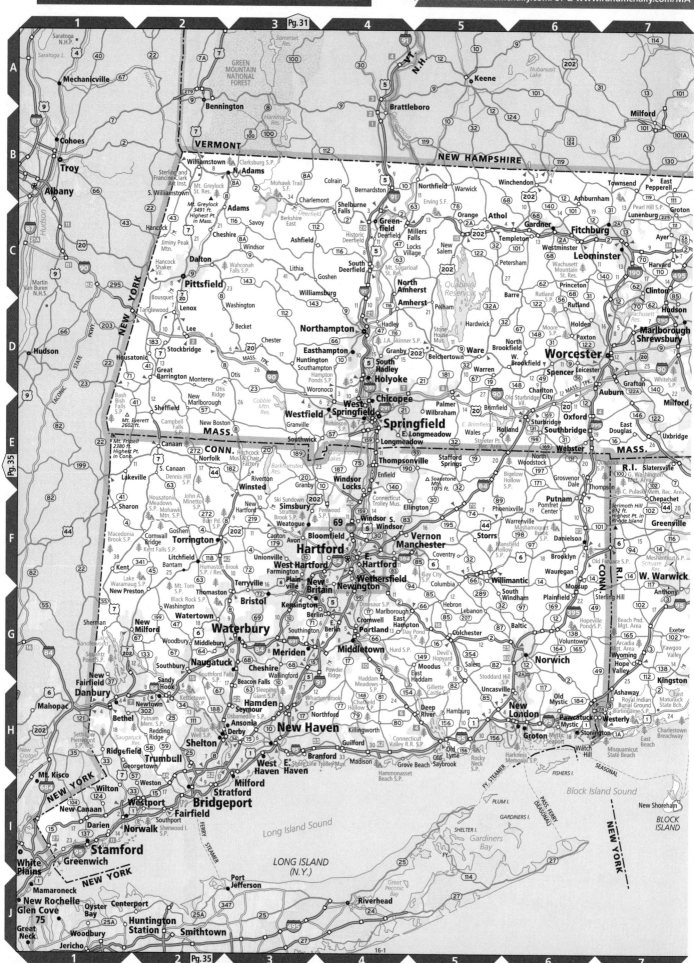

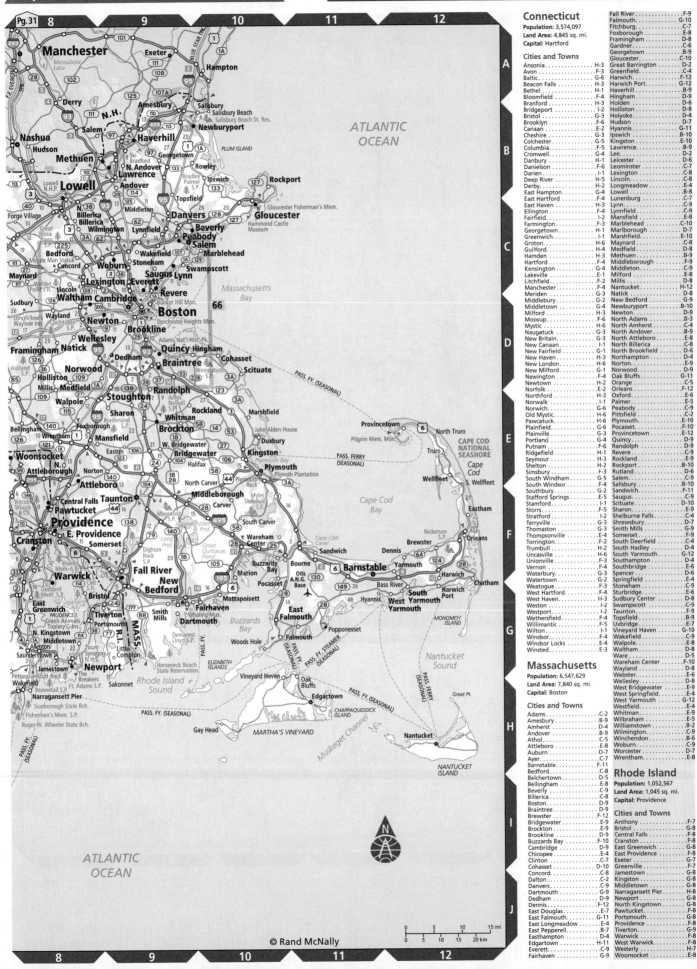

© Rand McNally

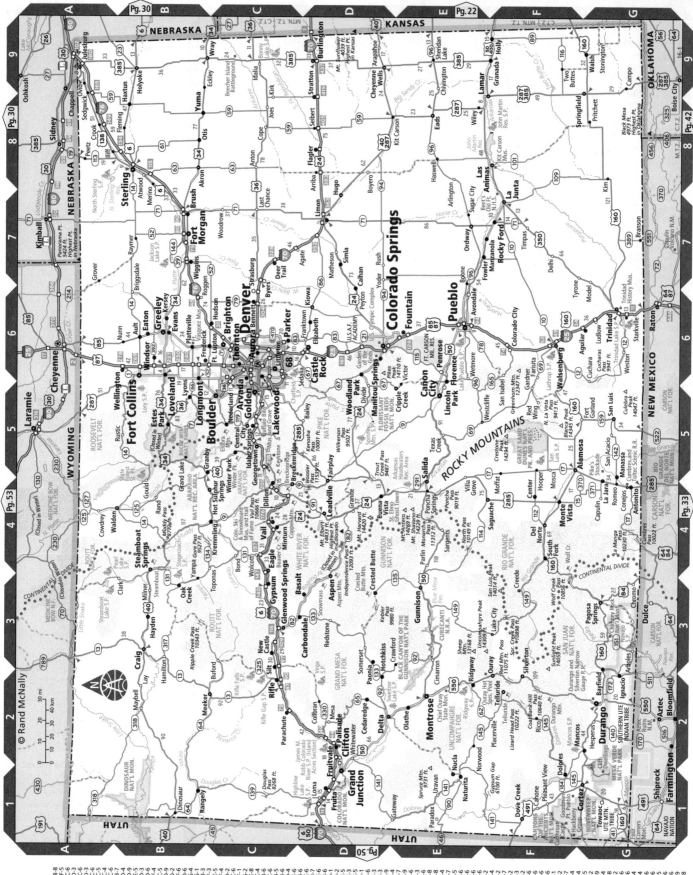

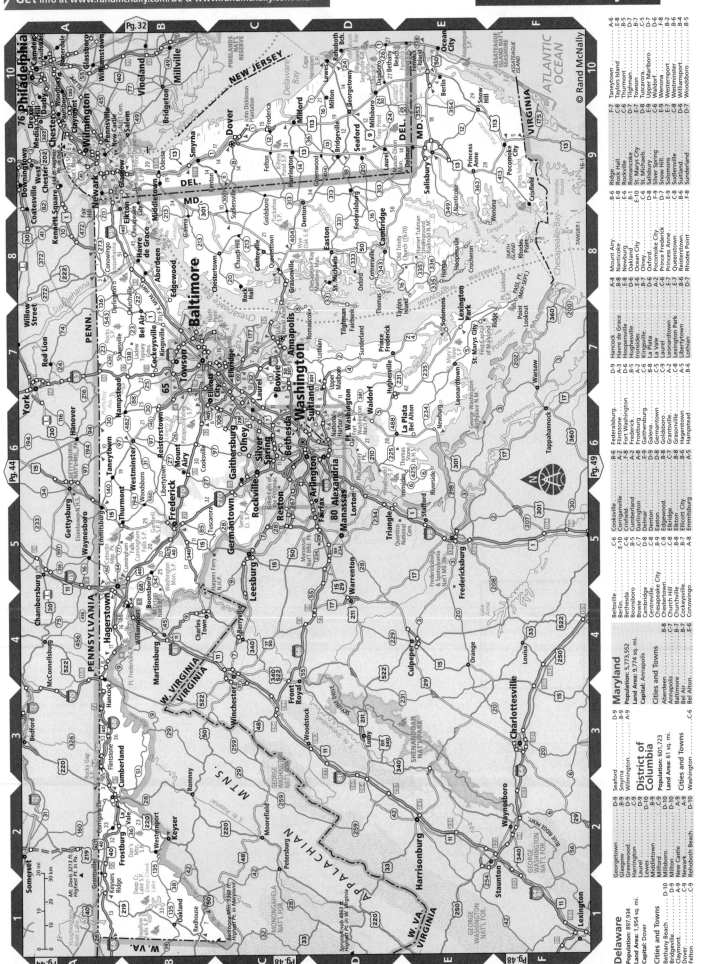

© Rand McNally

Florida

Population: 18,801,310
Land Area: 53,927 sq. mi.
Capital: Tallahassee

© Rand McNally

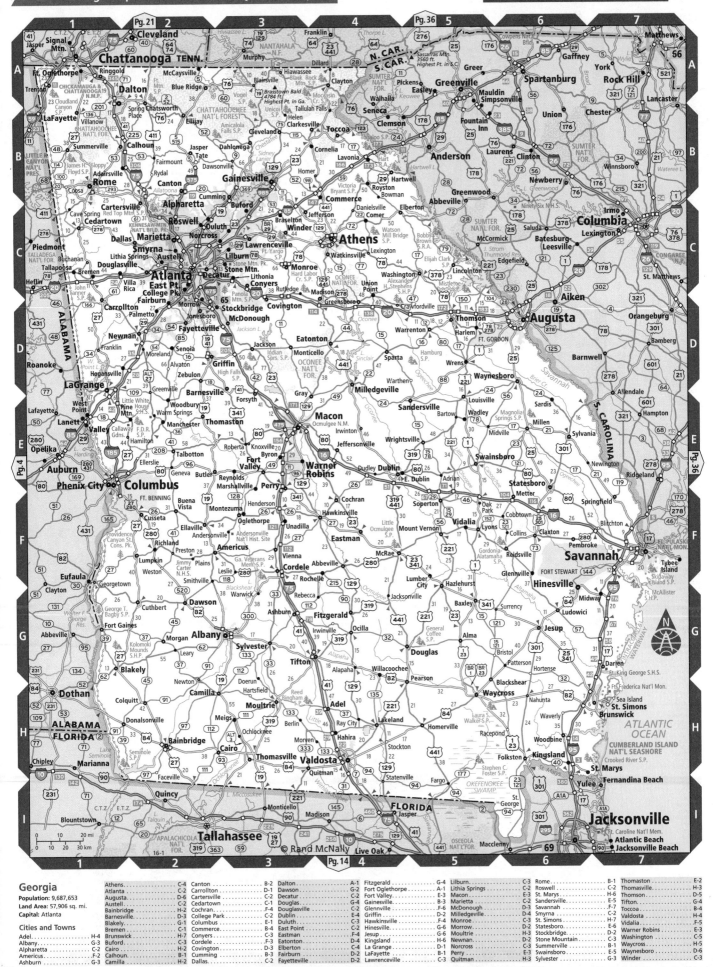

© Rand McNally

Idaho

Population: 1,567,582
Land Area: 82,747 sq. mi.
Capital: Boise

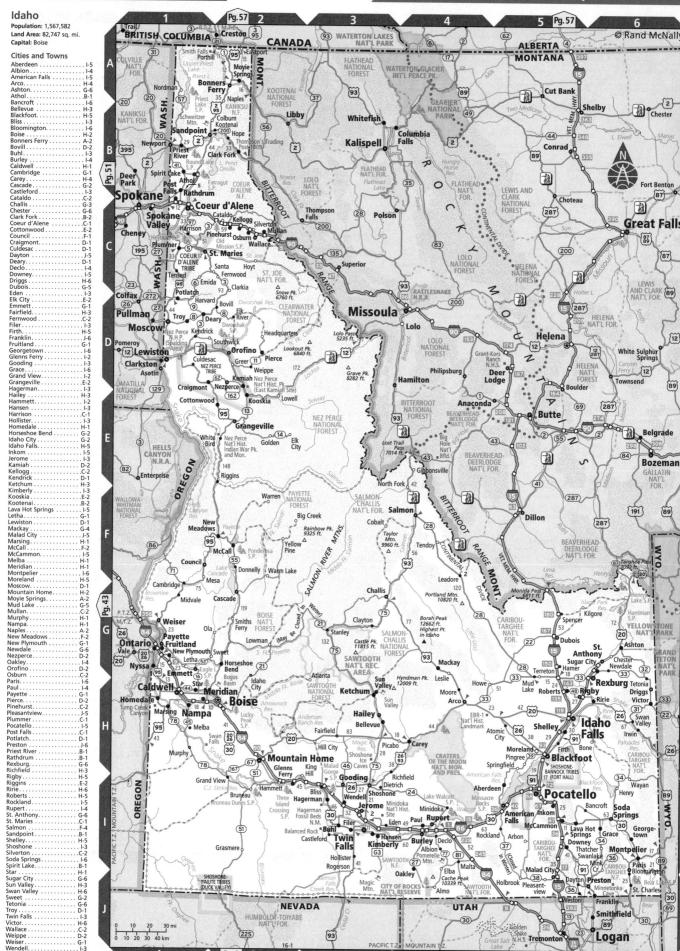

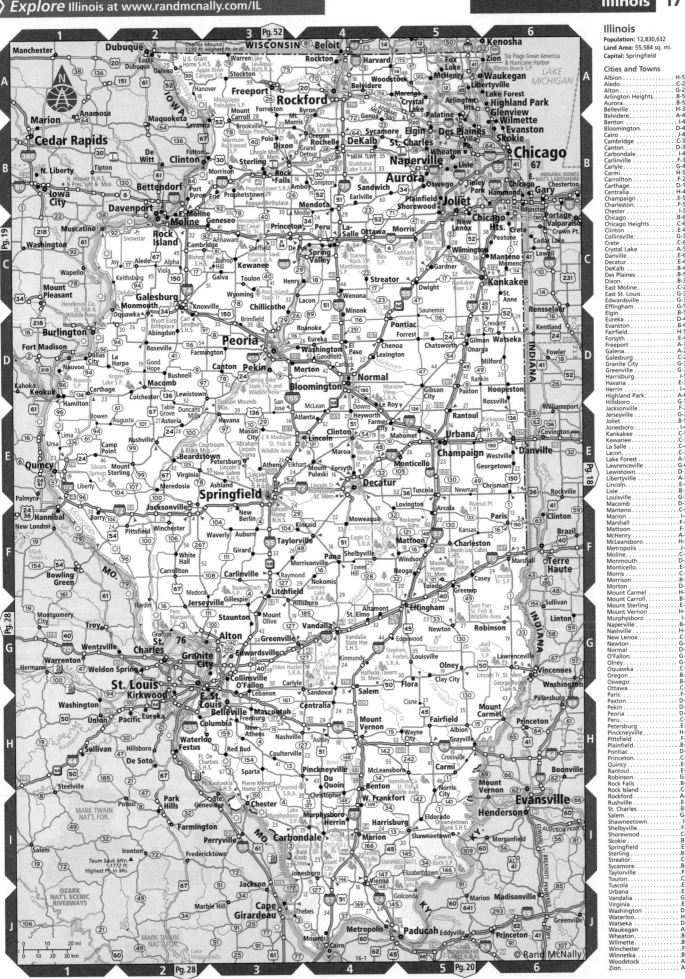

Illinois
Population: 12,830,632
Land Area: 55,584 sq. mi.
Capital: Springfield

© Rand McNally

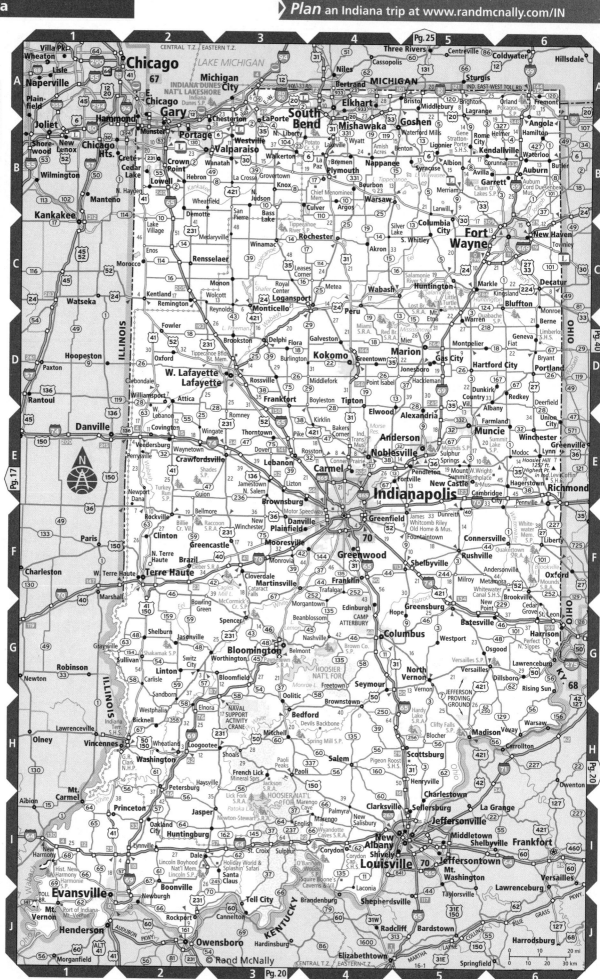

© Rand McNally

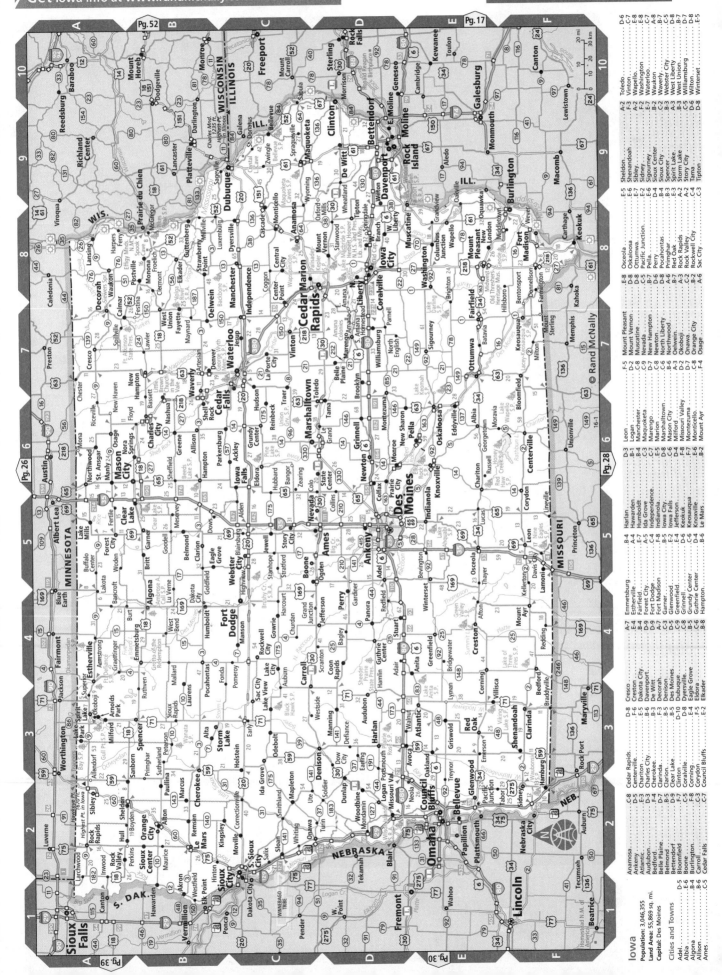

© Rand McNally

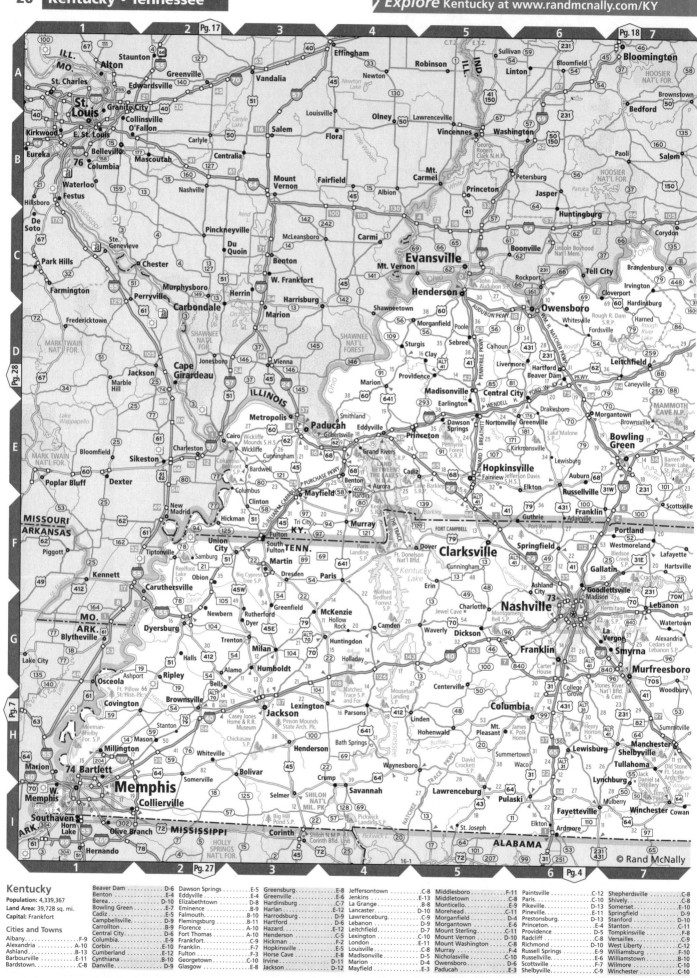

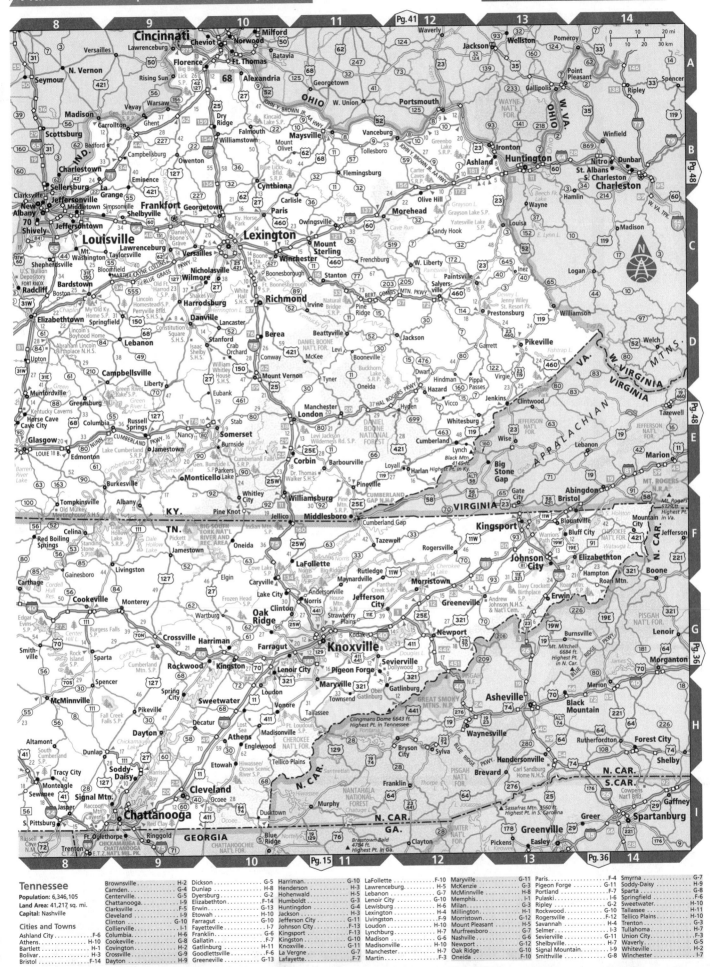

Kansas

Population: 2,853,118
Land Area: 81,815 sq. mi.
Capital: Topeka

Cities and Towns

Louisiana

Population: 4,533,372
Land Area: 43,562 sq. mi.
Capital: Baton Rouge

Maine

Population: 1,328,361
Land Area: 30,862 sq. mi.
Capital: Augusta

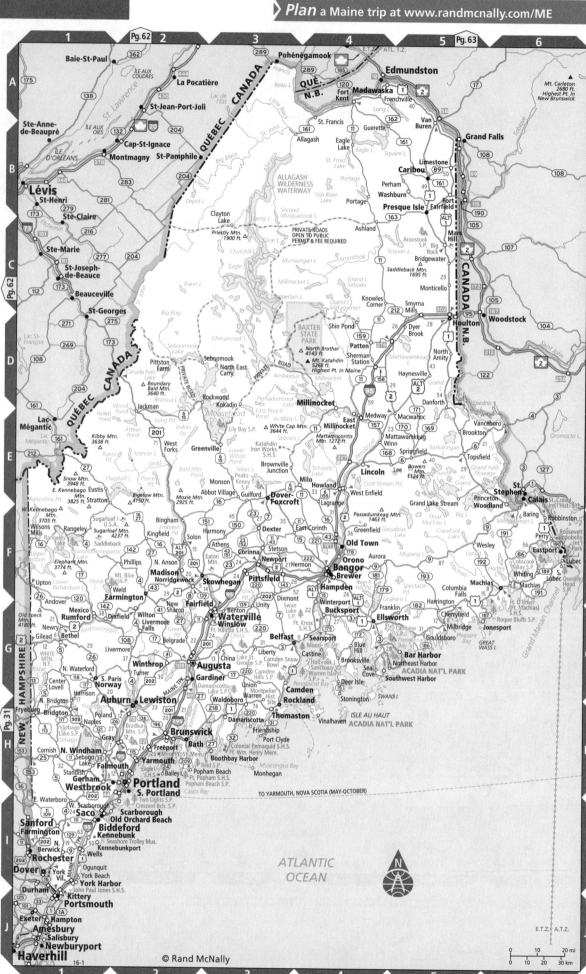

© Rand McNally

16-1

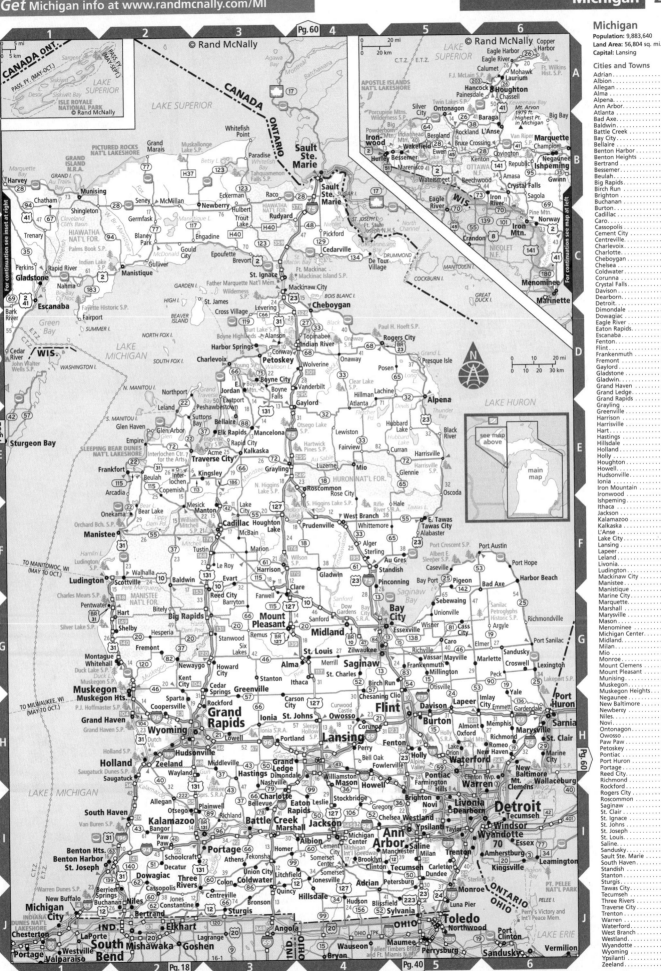

Michigan
Population: 9,883,640
Land Area: 56,804 sq. mi.
Capital: Lansing

Minnesota
Population: 5,303,925
Land Area: 79,610 sq. mi.
Capital: St. Paul

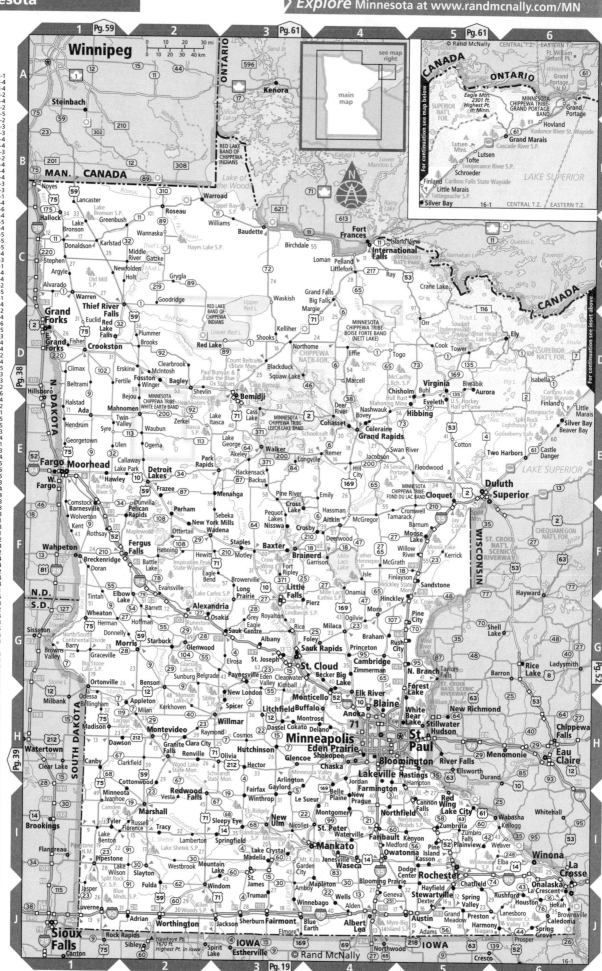

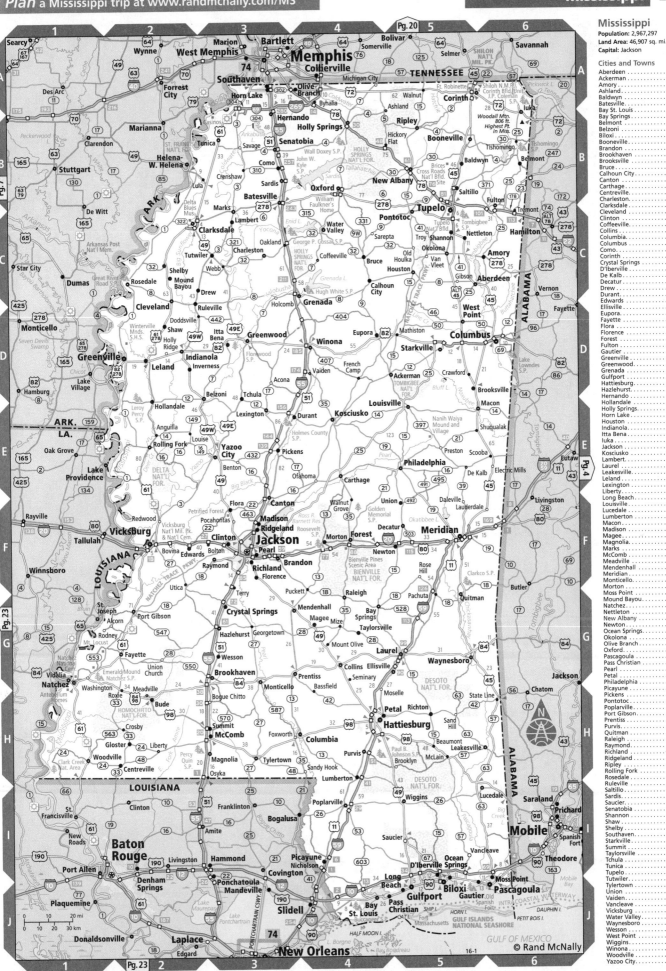

Pg. 20

Pg. 7

Pg. 23

Pg. 4

Pg. 23

Mississippi
Population: 2,967,297
Land Area: 46,907 sq. mi.
Capital: Jackson

© Rand McNally

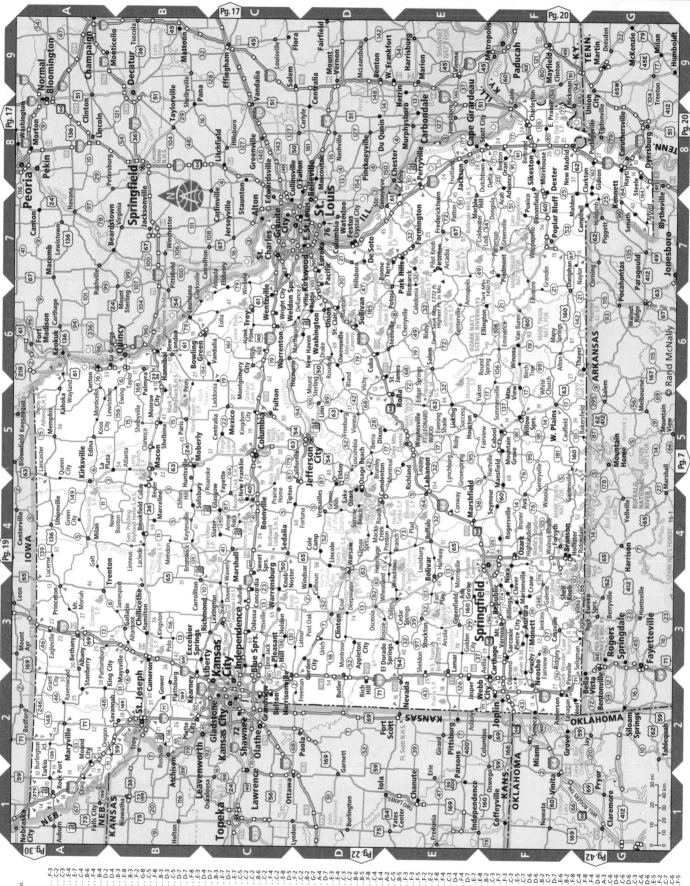

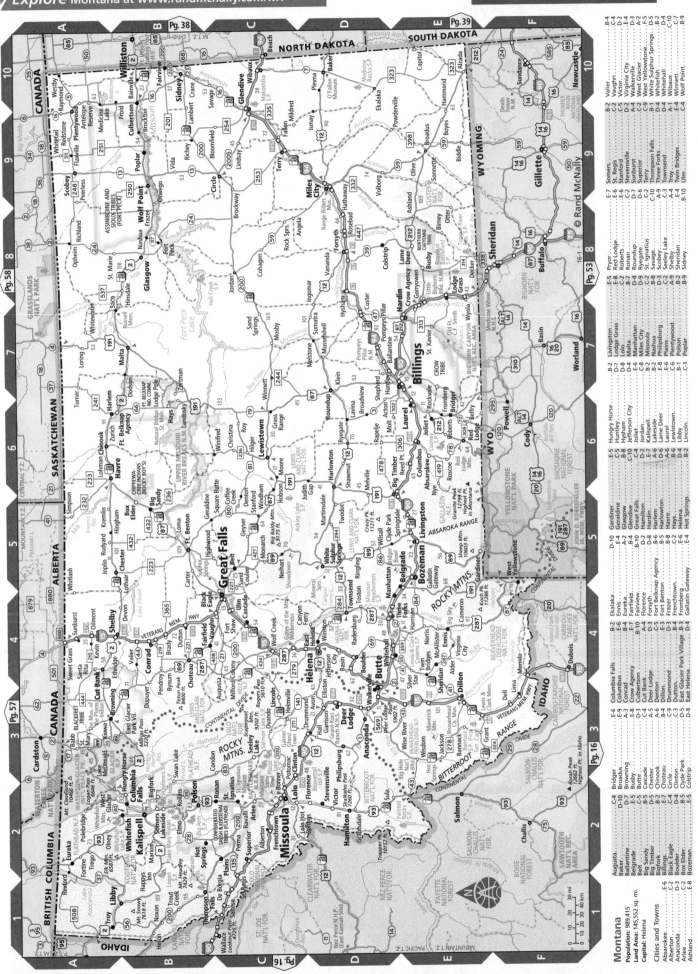

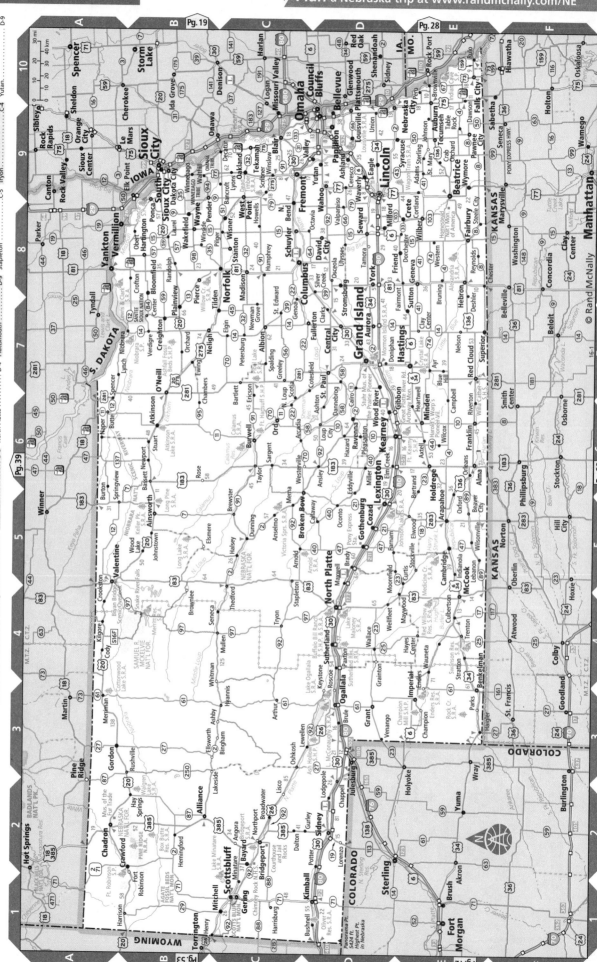

© Rand McNally

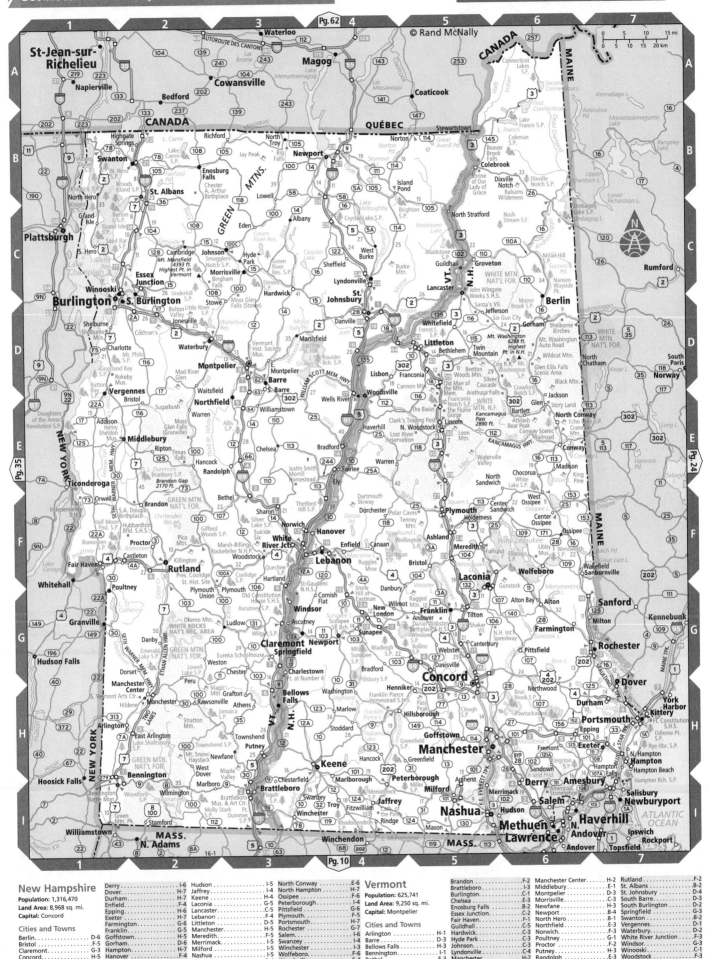

New Hampshire

Population: 1,316,470
Land Area: 8,968 sq. mi.
Capital: Concord

Cities and Towns

Vermont

Population: 625,741
Land Area: 9,250 sq. mi.
Capital: Montpelier

Cities and Towns

Explore New Jersey at www.randmcnally.com/NJ

New Jersey

Population: 8,791,894
Land Area: 7,417 sq. mi.
Capital: Trenton

Cities and Towns

© Rand McNally

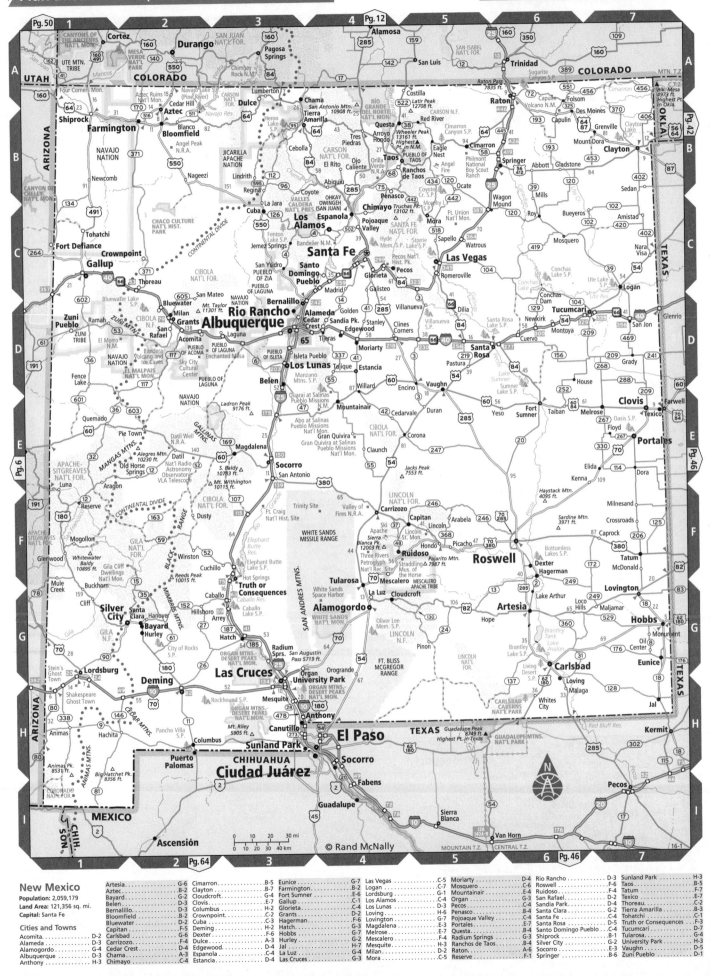

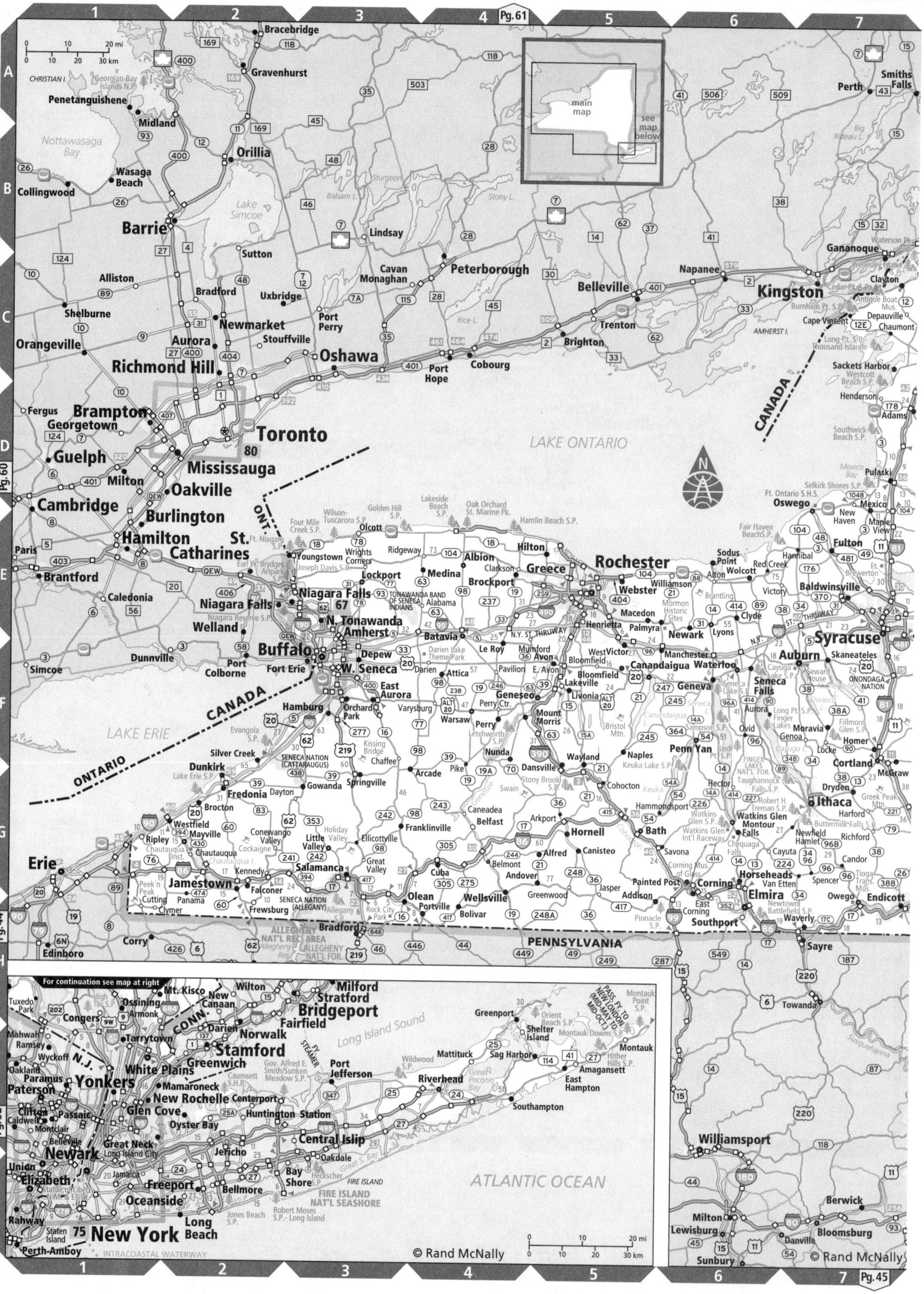

Pg. 61

main map

see map below

CHRISTIAN I.
Georgian Bay Islands N.P.
Nottawasaga Bay

Penetanguishene
Midland
Wasaga Beach
Collingwood
Barrie
Orillia
Bracebridge
Gravenhurst
Sutton
Alliston
Bradford
Uxbridge
Shelburne
Newmarket
Stouffville
Port Perry
Aurora
Orangeville
Richmond Hill
Oshawa
Port Hope
Cobourg
Fergus
Brampton
Georgetown
Guelph
Mississauga
Toronto
Oakville
Milton
Cambridge
Burlington
Hamilton
Paris
St. Catharines
Brantford
Caledonia
Niagara Falls
Welland
Dunnville
Buffalo
Simcoe
Port Colborne
Lindsay
Cavan Monaghan
Peterborough
Belleville
Trenton
Brighton
Napanee
Kingston
Cape Vincent
Clayton
Gananoque
Perth
Smiths Falls
Sackets Harbor
Henderson
Adams
Pulaski
Oswego
Mexico
New Haven
Fulton

LAKE ONTARIO
LAKE ERIE
ONTARIO
CANADA

Olcott
Youngstown
Niagara Falls
N. Tonawanda
Amherst
Depew
W. Seneca
East Aurora
Orchard Park
Hamburg
Silver Creek
Dunkirk
Fredonia
Brocton
Westfield
Mayville
Ripley
Erie
Jamestown
Falconer
Salamanca
Lockport
Medina
Brockport
Albion
Greece
Rochester
Webster
Henrietta
Batavia
Le Roy
Attica
Warsaw
Arcade
Springville
Gowanda
Little Valley
Ellicottville
Great Valley
Olean
Wellsville
Bolivar
Hilton
Ridgeway
Clarkson
Macedon
Palmyra
Newark
Lyons
Clyde
Canandaigua
Waterloo
Geneva
Seneca Falls
Auburn
Syracuse
Skaneateles
Manchester
Livonia
Geneseo
Mount Morris
Nunda
Dansville
Wayland
Naples
Penn Yan
Ovid
Moravia
Genoa
Locke
Homer
Cortland
McGraw
Dryden
Ithaca
Hornell
Canisteo
Bath
Hammondsport
Watkins Glen
Montour Falls
Horseheads
Elmira
Corning
Painted Post
Addison
Waverly
Sayre
Towanda
Williamsport
Berwick
Bloomsburg
Danville
Milton
Lewisburg
Sunbury

PENNSYLVANIA

ATLANTIC OCEAN
Long Island Sound

For continuation see map at right

Tuxedo Park
Mahwah
Ramsey
Wyckoff
Oakland
Paramus
Paterson
Clifton
Passaic
Montclair
Belleville
Newark
Union
Elizabeth
Rahway
Perth-Amboy
Staten Island
New York
Yonkers
White Plains
Mamaroneck
New Rochelle
Glen Cove
Oyster Bay
Great Neck
Long Island City
Jamaica
Freeport
Oceanside
Long Beach
Bellmore
Bay Shore
Central Islip
Oakdale
Jericho
Huntington Station
Centerport
Congers
Ossining
Armonk
Mt. Kisco
New Canaan
Darien
Norwalk
Fairfield
Bridgeport
Stratford
Milford
Wilton
Stamford
Greenwich
Tarrytown
Port Jefferson
Riverhead
Mattituck
Sag Harbor
Greenport
Shelter Island
Southampton
East Hampton
Amagansett
Montauk
FIRE ISLAND NAT'L SEASHORE
INTRACOASTAL WATERWAY

© Rand McNally

Pg. 44
Pg. 45
Pg. 60
Pg. 32

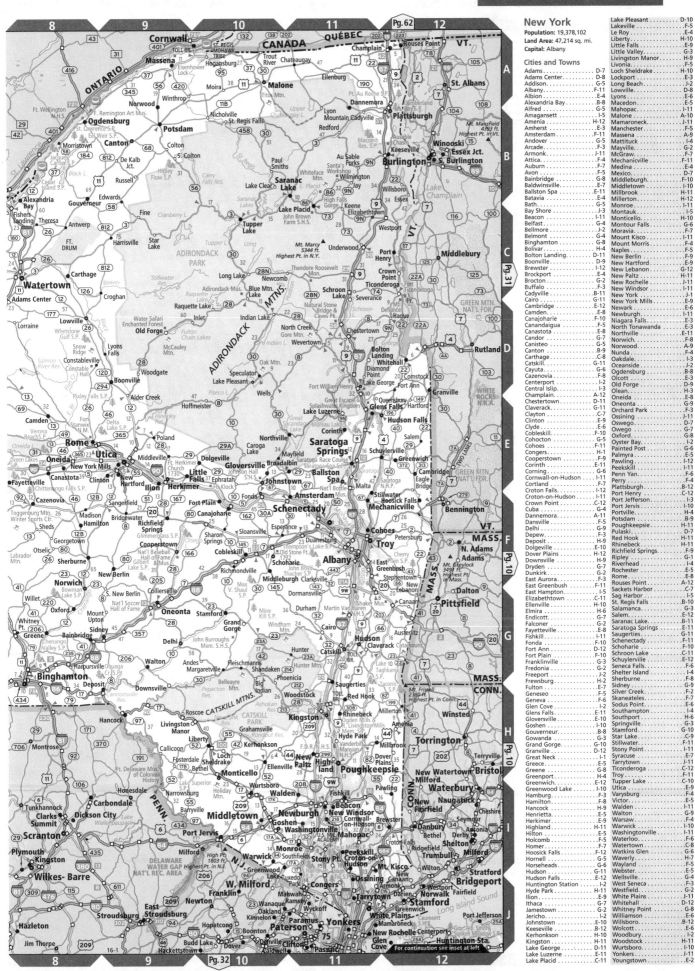

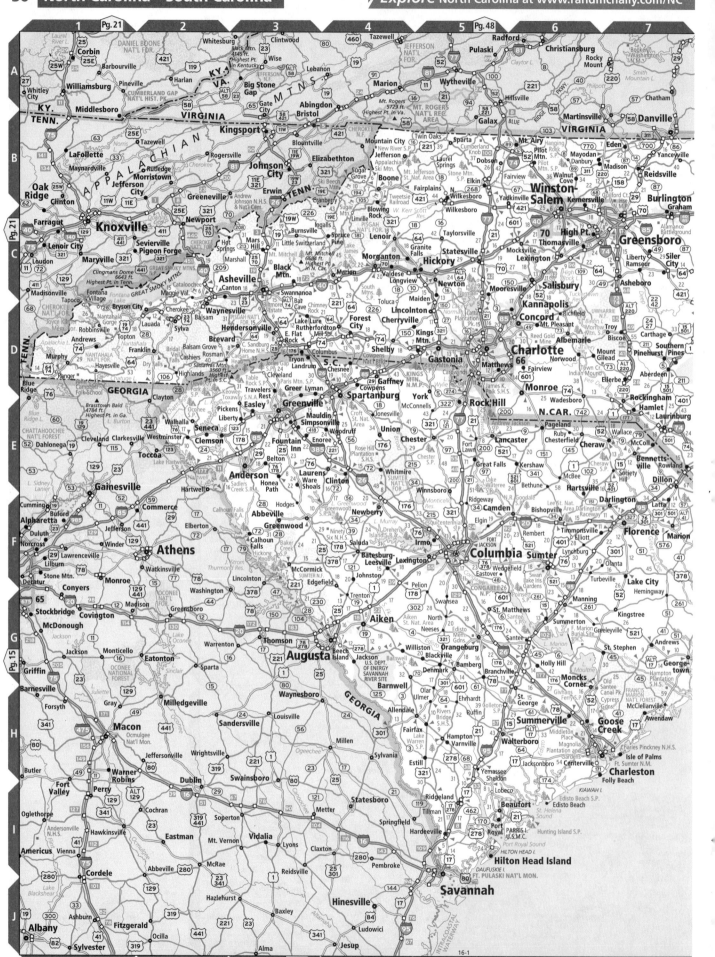

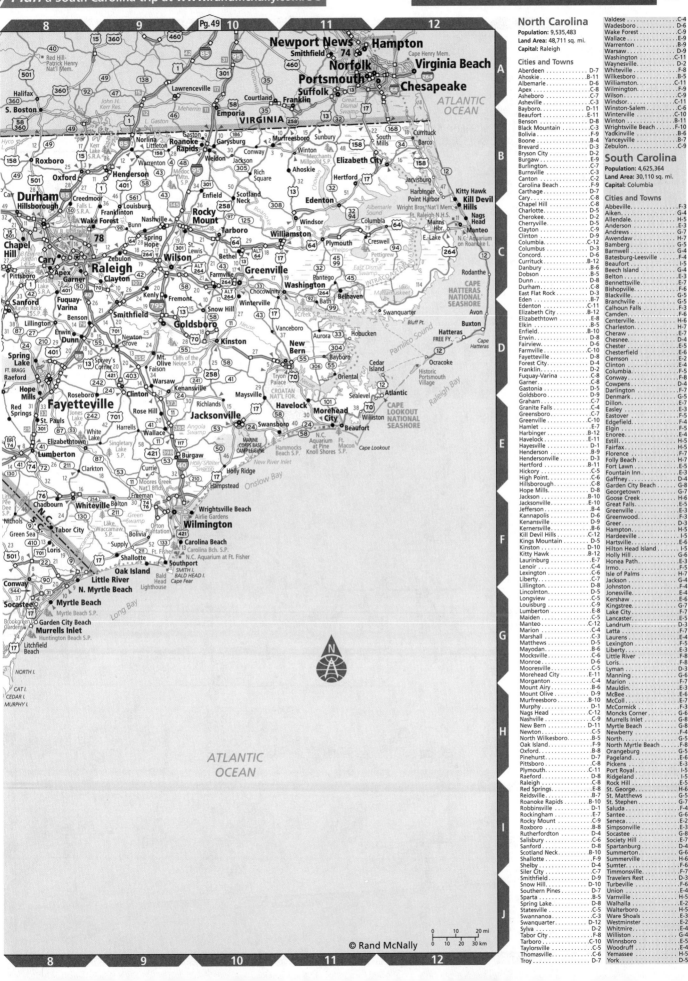

North Dakota

Population: 672,591
Land Area: 68,976 sq. mi.
Capital: Bismarck

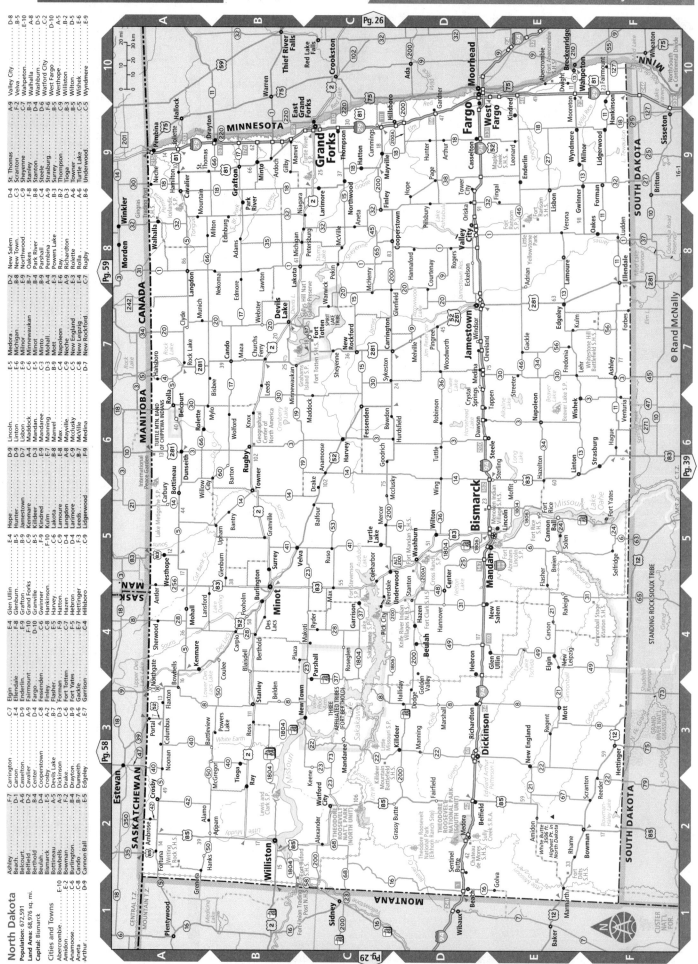

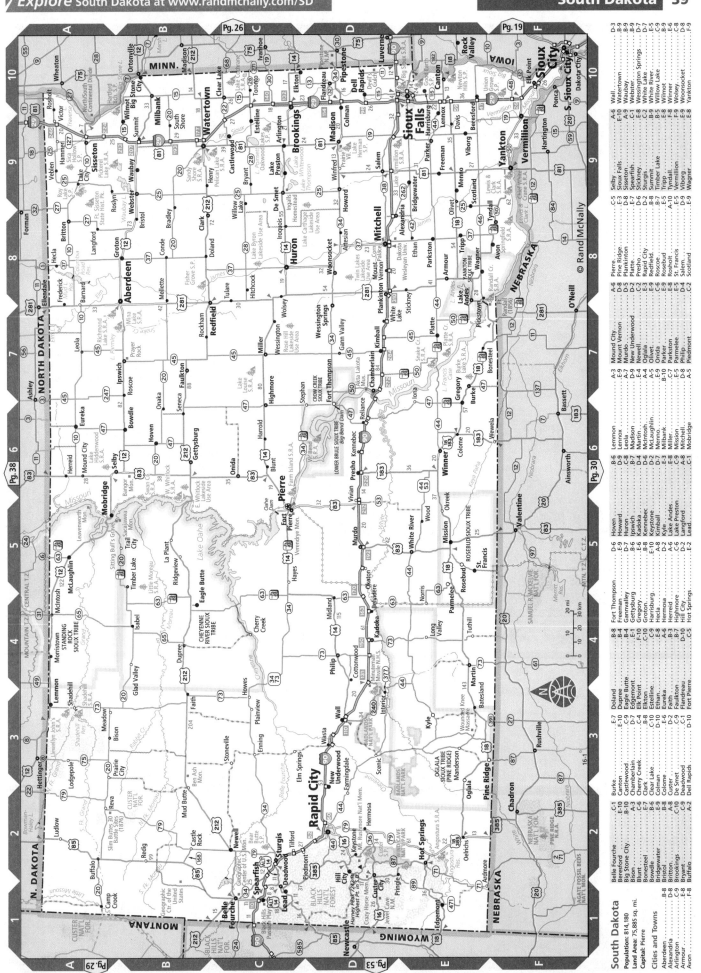

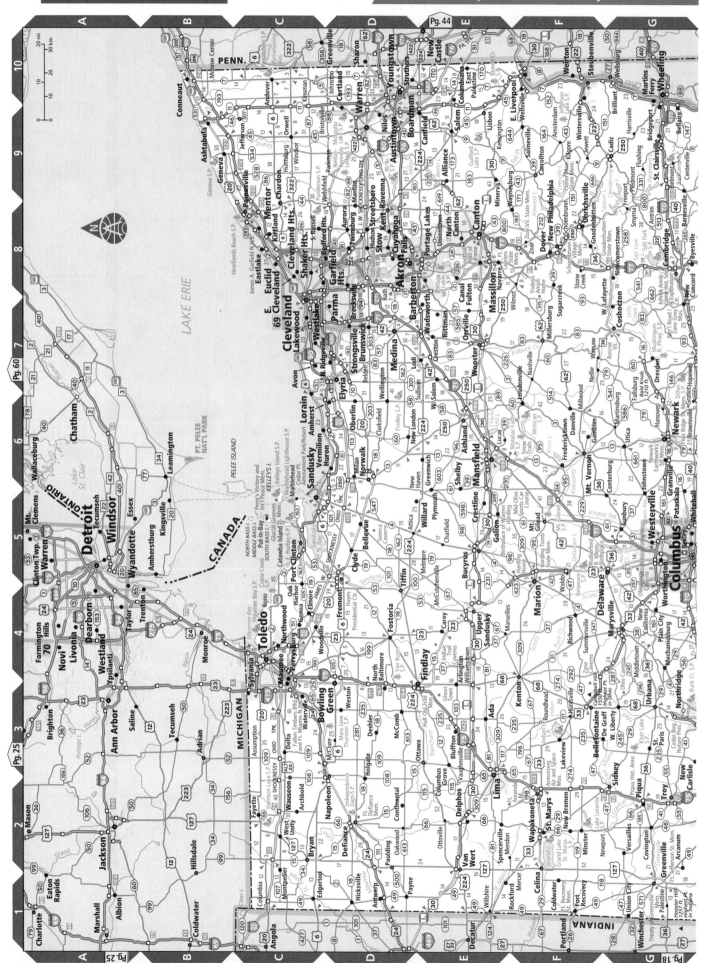

PENN.
W. VA.

© Rand McNally

Ohio

Population: 11,536,504
Land Area: 40,948 sq. mi.
Capital: Columbus

Cities and Towns

Aberdeen	K-3
Ada	E-3
Akron	D-8
Alliance	D-9
Amherst	C-6
Antwerp	D-1
Arcanum	F-2
Archbold	C-2
Ashland	D-6
Ashtabula	B-9
Athens	G-6
Aurora	C-8
Austintown	D-9
Avon	C-6
Baltimore	F-5
Barberton	D-8
Barnesville	F-8
Batavia	H-3
Beavercreek	G-2

Bedford Heights	D-8
Bellaire	F-9
Bellefontaine	F-3
Bellevue	C-5
Belmont	F-8
Belpre	G-7
Bethel	H-3
Bexley	F-5
Blanchester	G-3
Blue Ash	H-2
Bluffton	E-3
Boardman	D-9
Boston Heights	D-8
Bowling Green	C-3
Brecksville	C-8
Bridgeport	F-9
Brookville	F-2
Brunswick	C-7
Bryan	C-1
Bucyrus	E-5
Byesville	F-7
Cadiz	E-8
Caldwell	F-7
Cambridge	F-7
Camden	H-1

Canal Fulton	D-8
Canfield	D-9
Canton	D-8
Carey	D-4
Carroll	F-5
Carrollton	E-8
Cedarville	G-3
Celina	E-2
Centerville	G-2
Chardon	C-8
Cheviot	H-2
Chillicothe	G-4
Circleville	F-5
Cincinnati	H-2
Cleveland	C-8
Cleveland Heights	C-8
Cleves	H-1
Coldwater	E-2
Columbiana	D-9
Columbus	F-5
Columbus Grove	E-3
Conneaut	B-10
Cortland	C-9
Coshocton	E-7
Covington	F-2
Crestline	D-5

Creston	E-8
Crooksville	F-6
Cuyahoga Falls	D-8
Dayton	G-2
Defiance	D-2
Delaware	F-4
Delphos	E-2
Delta	C-2
Dover	E-8
East Cleveland	C-8
East Liverpool	D-10
East Palestine	D-10
Eastlake	C-8
Eaton	G-1
Edgerton	C-1
Edon	C-1
Elyria	C-6
Englewood	F-2
Euclid	C-8
Fairborn	G-2
Fairfield	H-1
Fayette	C-2
Findlay	D-3
Forest Park	H-2
Fostoria	D-4
Frankfort	G-4
Fredericktown	E-5
Fremont	C-4

Gallipolis	H-6
Gambier	E-6
Garfield Heights	D-8
Genoa	C-3
Georgetown	H-3
Germantown	G-2
Greenfield	G-4
Greensburg	D-8
Greentown	D-8
Greenville	F-1
Greenwich	D-6
Hamilton	H-1
Hamler	D-2
Harrison	H-1
Hartville	D-8
Hicksville	D-1
Hillsboro	G-3
Hubbard	C-9
Hudson	D-8
Ironton	J-5
Jackson	H-5
Jamestown	G-3
Jefferson	B-9
Johnstown	F-5
Kent	D-8
Kenton	E-4
Kettering	G-2
Kirtland	C-8

Lakewood	K-7
Lancaster	F-6
Lebanon	G-2
Lima	E-3
Lisbon	D-9
Lodi	D-7
Logan	G-6
London	G-4
Lorain	C-6
Loudonville	D-6
Loveland	H-2
Lucasville	J-5
Mansfield	D-6
Mantua	D-8
Maple Heights	C-8
Marietta	G-7
Marion	E-5
Martins Ferry	F-9
Marysville	F-4
Mason	H-2
Massillon	D-8
Maumee	C-3
McArthur	G-5
McComb	D-3
McConnelsville	F-7
Mechanicsburg	F-3

Medina	C-7
Mentor	C-8
Miamisburg	G-2
Middleport	H-6
Middletown	G-2
Milford	H-2
Millersburg	E-7
Minerva	D-8
Minster	E-2
Montpelier	C-1
Mount Gilead	E-5
Mount Orab	H-3
Mount Sterling	G-4
Mount Vernon	E-5
Napoleon	C-2
Nelsonville	G-6
New Boston	J-5
New Bremen	E-2
New Carlisle	F-2
New Concord	F-7
New Lebanon	G-2
New Lexington	F-6
New London	D-6
New Paris	G-1
New Philadelphia	E-8
New Richmond	J-2

Newark	D-7
Newcomerstown	E-7
Niles	C-9
North Baltimore	D-3
North Canton	D-8
North College Hill	H-2
North Ridgeville	C-7
Northwood	C-3
Norton	D-8
Norwalk	C-6
Norwood	H-2
Oak Harbor	C-4
Oak Hill	H-5
Oberlin	C-6
Orrville	D-7
Orwell	C-9
Oxford	H-1
Painesville	C-8
Parma	C-7
Pataskala	F-5
Paulding	D-2
Peebles	H-3
Perrysburg	C-3
Piketon	J-4
Piqua	F-2
Plain City	F-4

Plymouth	D-5
Pomeroy	H-6
Port Clinton	C-4
Portage Lakes	D-8
Portsmouth	K-5
Powhatan Point	F-9
Ravenna	D-8
Reading	H-2
Richwood	E-4
Ripley	J-3
Rittman	D-7
St. Clairsville	F-8
St. Marys	E-2
Salem	D-9
Sandusky	C-5
Sebring	D-9
Shaker Heights	C-8
Shelby	D-6
Sidney	F-2
Solon	C-8
Somerset	F-6
South Charleston	G-3
South Lebanon	H-2
South Russell	C-8
Spencerville	E-2
Springfield	F-3
Steubenville	E-9
Stow	D-8

Streetsboro	D-8
Strongsville	C-7
Struthers	D-9
Sugarcreek	E-8
Sunbury	F-5
Sylvania	B-3
Tiffin	D-4
Tipp City	F-2
Toledo	C-3
Trenton	H-1
Trotwood	G-2
Troy	F-2
Twinsburg	D-8
Uhrichsville	E-8
Union City	F-1
Uniontown	D-8
Upper Sandusky	D-4
Urbana	F-3
Utica	E-6
Van Wert	E-2
Vandalia	F-2
Vermilion	C-6
Versailles	F-2
Wadsworth	D-7
Wapakoneta	E-3
Warren	C-9
Washington Ct. House	G-3
Waterville	C-3

Wauseon	C-2
Waverly	J-5
Wellington	D-6
Wellston	G-5
Wellsville	E-10
West Lafayette	E-7
West Liberty	F-3
West Salem	D-7
West Union	J-2
West Unity	C-1
Westerville	F-5
Westlake	C-7
Weston	C-3
Whitehall	F-5
Willard	D-5
Williamsburg	H-3
Williamsport	G-4
Willoughby	C-8
Wilmington	G-3
Winchester	H-2
Withamsville	H-2
Woodsfield	F-8
Wooster	D-7
Worthington	F-5
Xenia	G-2
Yellow Springs	F-2
Youngstown	D-9
Zanesville	F-6

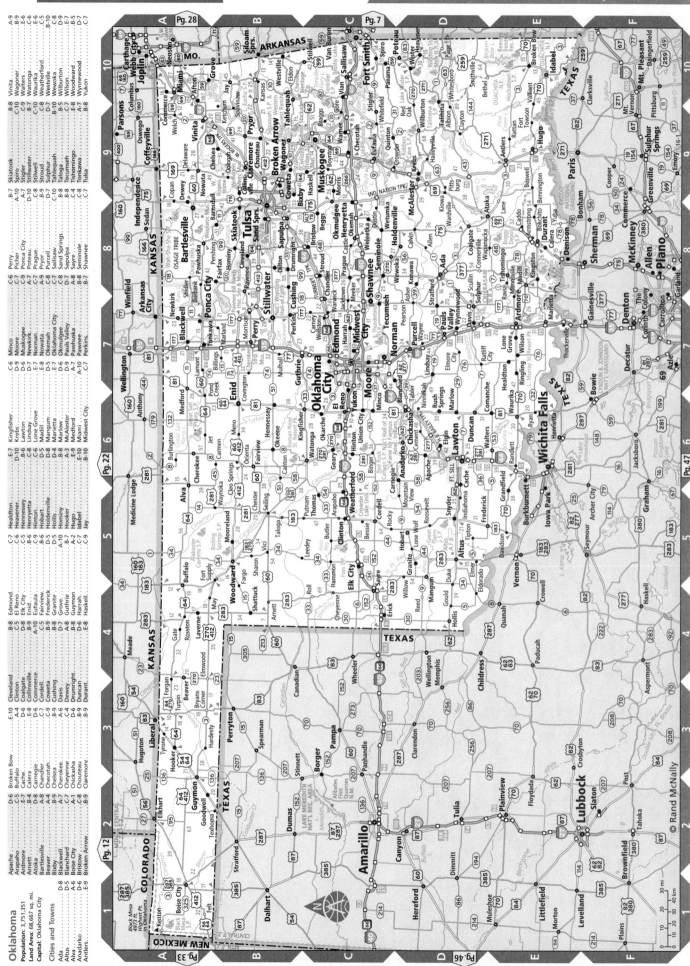

Oregon

Population: 3,831,074
Land Area: 95,997 sq. mi.
Capital: Salem

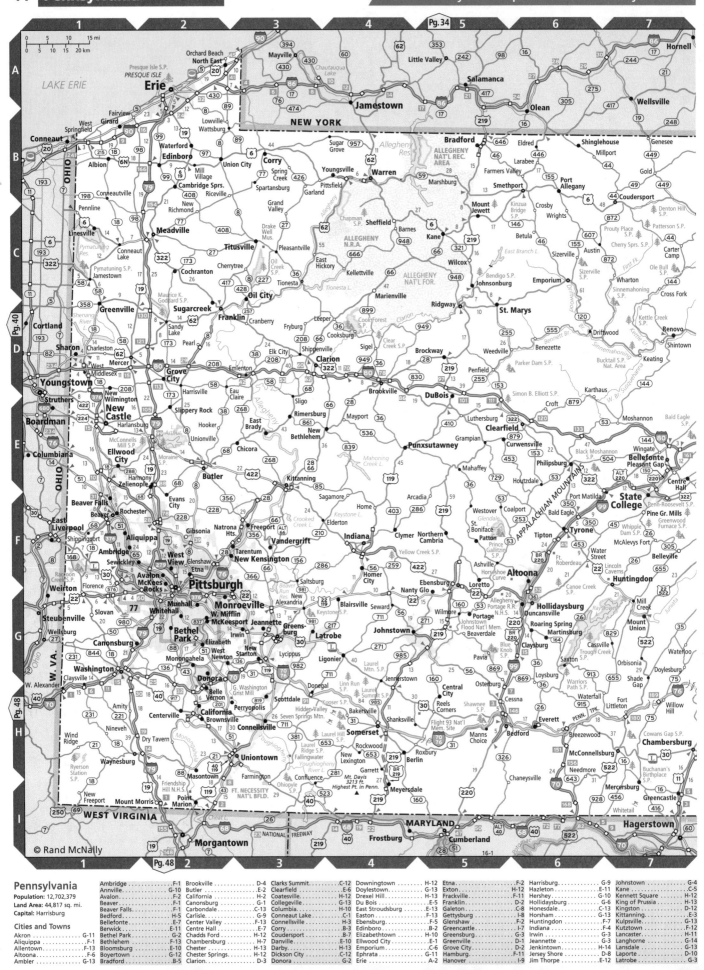

Pennsylvania

Population: 12,702,379
Land Area: 44,817 sq. mi.
Capital: Harrisburg

Cities and Towns

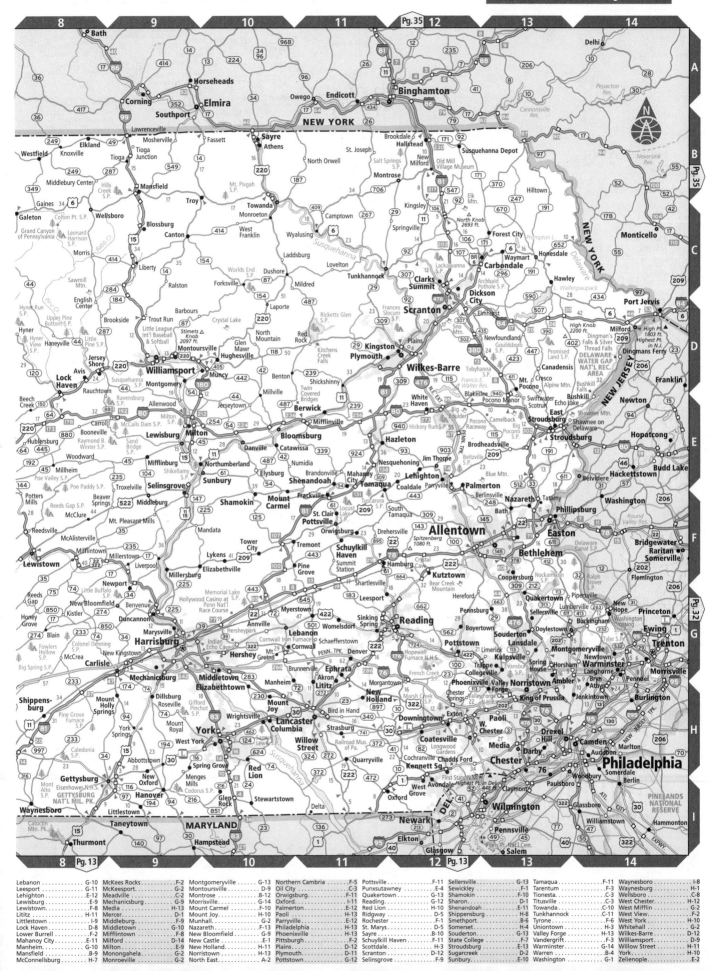

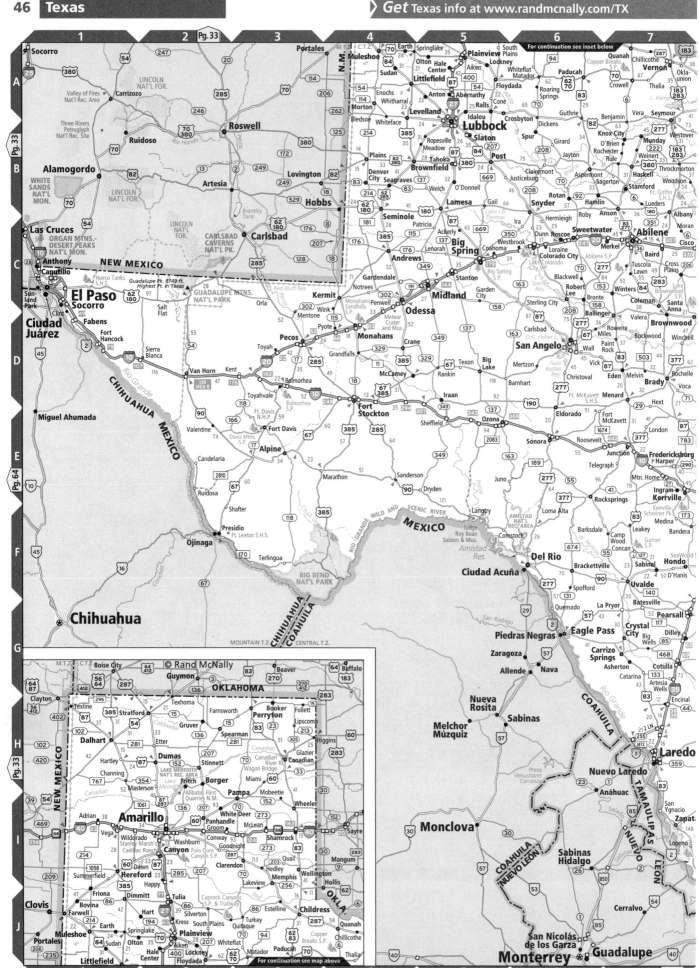

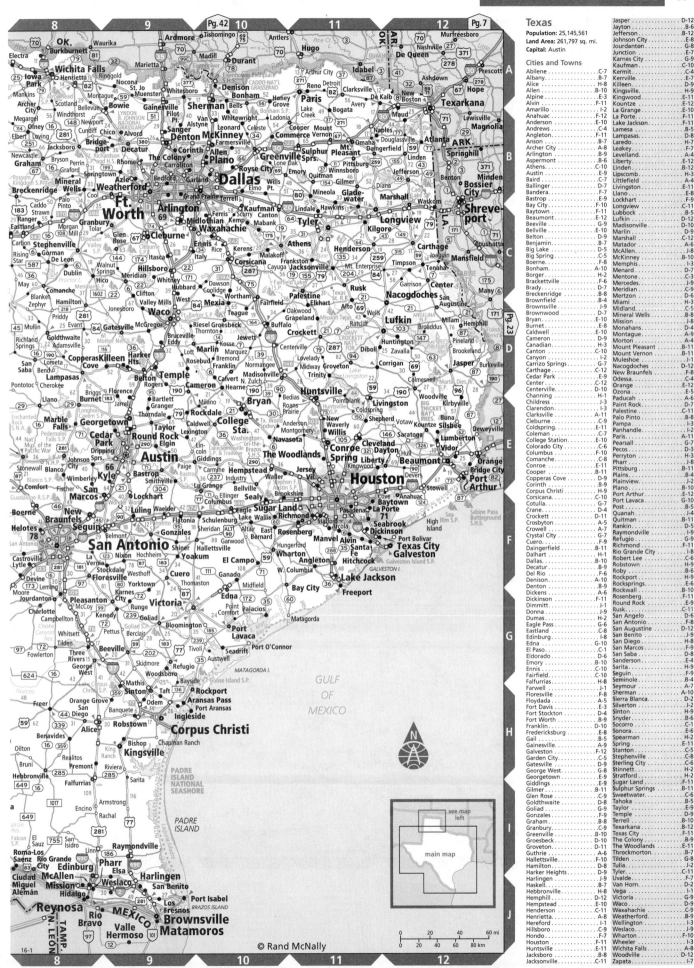

Cities and Towns

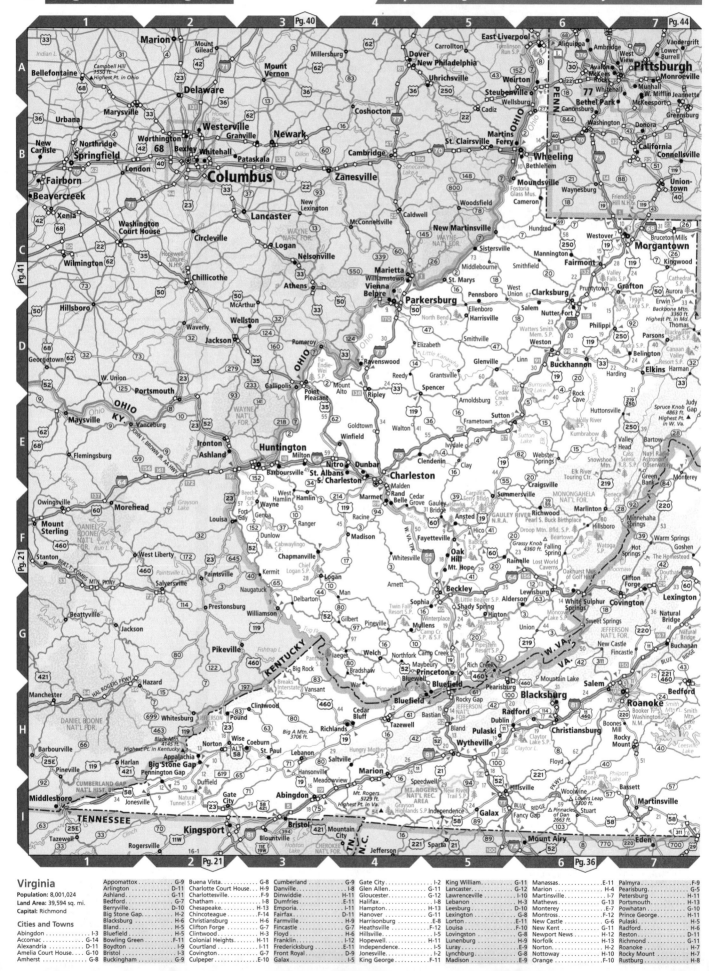

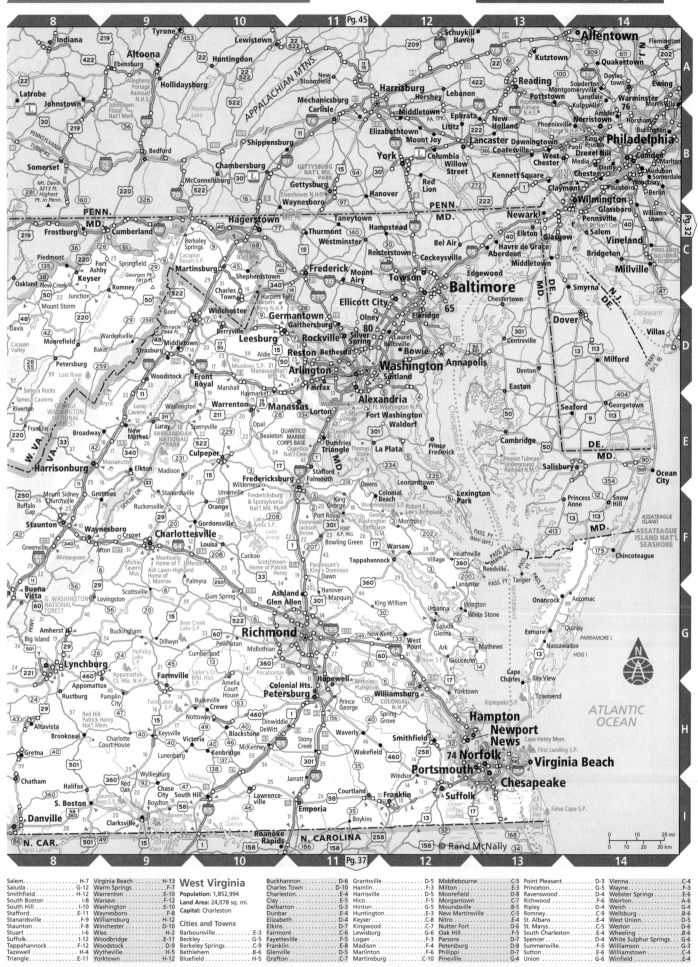

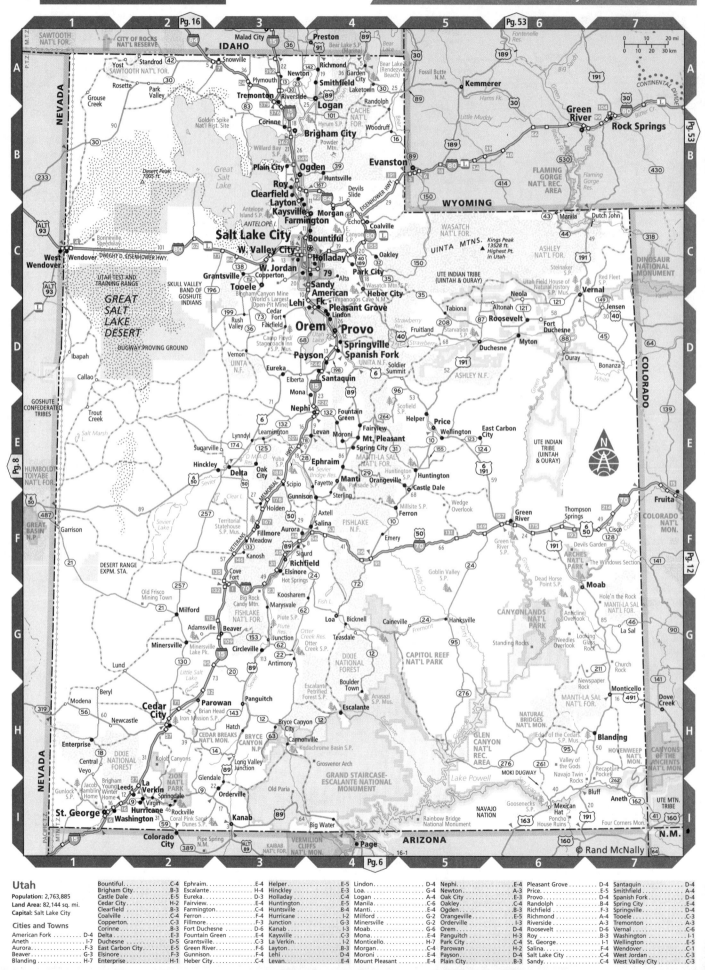

© Rand McNally

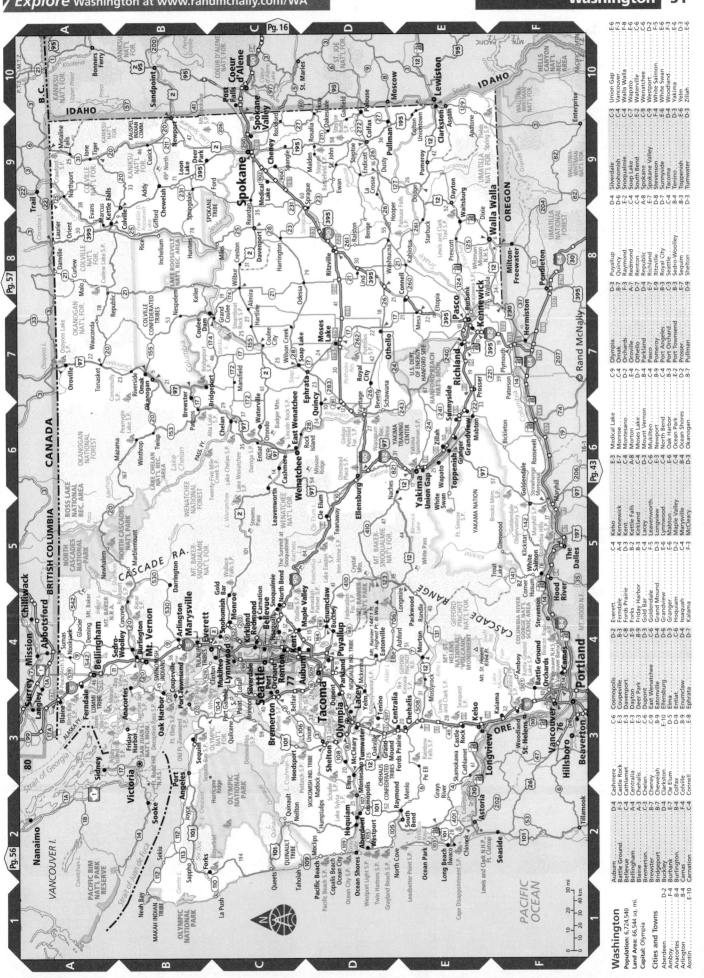

▶ *Plan* a Wisconsin trip at www.randmcnally.com/WI

Wisconsin

Population: 5,686,986
Land Area: 54,310 sq. mi.
Capital: Madison

Cities and Towns

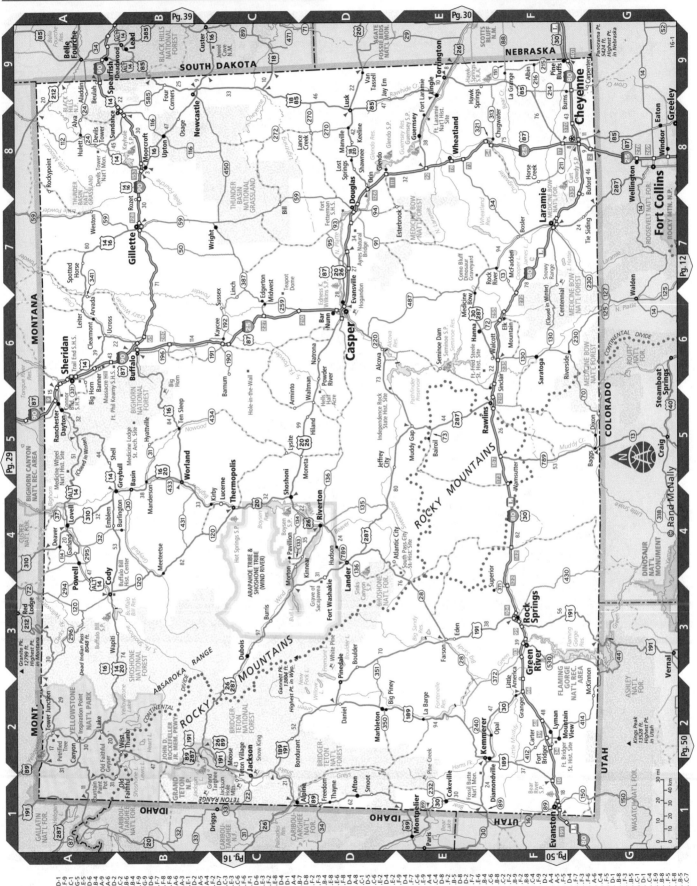

Wyoming

Population: 563,626
Land Area: 97,100 sq. mi.
Capital: Cheyenne

1 2 3 4 5 6 7

A B C D E F G H I J

ALASKA

Mt. McKinley (Denali) 20,320 ft. Highest Pt. in North America ▲

DENALI NAT'L PARK & PRES.

Fairbanks

YUKON-CHARLEY RIVERS NAT'L PRES.

ALASKA RANGE

WRANGELL-ST. ELIAS NAT'L PARK AND PRES.

Anchorage

Cordova

GLACIER BAY NAT'L PARK & PRES.

GULF OF ALASKA

CHICHAGOF ISLAND

BARANOF ISLAND

Juneau

ADMIRALTY ISLAND

PRINCE OF WALES ISLAND

Cape Knox

QUEEN CHARLOTTE ISLANDS

GWAII HAANAS NAT'L PARK RES.

Cape St. James

BANKS ISLAND

Cape Scott Prov. Park

VANCOUVER ISLAND

Campbell River

PACIFIC RIM N.P. RESERVE

PACIFIC OCEAN

Victoria

Seattle

Tacoma

Olympia

OLYMPIC N.P.

NORTH CASCADES N.P.

Portland

Salem

Eugene

Crater Lake Nat'l Pk.

OREGON

Lava Beds Nat'l Mon.

Lassen Volcanic N.P.

CALIF.

Sacramento

Reno

Carson City

YOSEMITE N.P.

NEVADA

UNITED STATES

IVVAVIK N.P.

VUNTUT N.P.

ARCTIC CIRCLE

PACIFIC TIME ZONE

ALASKA TIME ZONE

Dawson

YUKON

Haines Junction

Whitehorse

Watson Lake

PELLY MOUNTAINS

SELWYN MOUNTAINS

ROSS River

Mt. Logan 19,551 ft. Highest Pt. in Canada ▲

COAST MOUNTAINS

Stewart

Prince Rupert

Fort McPherson

Inuvik

Tuktoyaktuk

BEAUFORT SEA

Mackenzie

MACKENZIE MTS.

NÁÁTS'IHCH'OH N.P. RES.

NAHANNI N.P. RES.

CONTINENTAL DIVIDE

Fort Simpson

Wrigley

Fort Nelson

MUNCHO LAKE PROV. PARK

STONE MTN. PROV. PARK

NORTHWEST TERRITORIES

Yellowknife

Great Slave Lake

Ft. Providence

Hay River

Enterprise

Fort Smith

Fitzgerald

WOOD BUFFALO N.P.

Uranium City

Lake Athabasca

ATHABASCA SAND DUNES PROV. PARK

BANKS ISLAND MIGRATORY BIRD SANCTUARY

AULAVIK N.P.

Sachs Harbour

Cape Kellett

Cape Lambton

Cape Bathurst

Ulukhaktok

Amundsen Gulf

Dolphin and Union Strait

Coronation Gulf

Kugluktuk

VICTORIA ISLAND

Ikaluktutiak (Cambridge Bay)

Port Radium

Great Bear Lake

THELON WILDLIFE SANCTUARY

Aylmer L.

Baker L.

Dubawnt Lake

Nueltin Lake

MELVILLE ISLAND

Viscount Melville Sound

MOUNTAIN TIME ZONE

STEFANSSON ISLAND

Prince of Wales Strait

M'Clintock Channel

PRINCE OF WALES ISLAND

SOMERSET ISLAND

Boothia Peninsula

BATHURST ISLAND

CORNWALLIS ISLAND

Qausuittuq (Resolute)

CENTRAL TIME ZONE

Brodeur Peninsula

Tununirusiq (Arctic Bay)

Barrow Strait

Gulf of Boothia

Talurqjuak (Taloyoak)

KING WILLIAM ISLAND

Oqsuqtooq (Gjoa Haven)

Queen Maud Gulf

QUEEN MAUD GULF MIGRATORY BIRD SANCTUARY

ARCTIC CIRCLE

NUN...

Iglulgaarjuk (Chesterfield Inlet)

ALBERTA

Fort MacKay

Ft. McMurray

La Loche

CLEARWATER RIVER PROV. PARK

GREGOIRE LAKE PROV. PARK

Edmonton

St. Paul

Lloydminster

Red Deer

Rocky Mountain House

JASPER N.P.

Jasper

Hinton

Whitecourt

Valleyview

Peace River

Grande Prairie

Dawson Creek

Chetwynd

BRITISH COLUMBIA

COAST MOUNTAINS

Bella Coola

Williams Lake

Quesnel

Prince George

Campbell River

Kamloops

Vancouver

Penticton

Cranbrook

Kimberley

Banff

Calgary

BANFF N.P.

ROCKY MOUNTAINS

SELKIRK MTS.

WELLS GRAY PROV. PARK

BOWRON LAKE PROV. PARK

Brooks

Medicine Hat

Lethbridge

WATERTON LAKES N.P.

WATERTON-GLACIER INT'L PEACE PARK

GLACIER N.P.

LEWIS RANGE

BITTERROOT RANGE

Spokane

WASH.

Missoula

Lewiston

Helena

Butte

Great Falls

Billings

MONTANA

IDAHO

Boise

Pocatello

Craters of the Moon Nat'l Mon.

Newberry Nat'l Volcanic Mon.

CASCADE RANGE

Great Salt Lake

Ogden

Salt Lake City

UTAH

DINOSAUR NAT'L MON.

CONTINENTAL DIVIDE

WYOMING

YELLOWSTONE N.P.

GRAND TETON N.P.

Pathfinder Reservoir

Casper

Cheyenne

COLO.

SASKATCHEWAN

CLEARWATER RIVER PROV. PARK

Wollaston Lake

LAC LA RONGE PROV. PARK

MEADOW LAKE PROV. PARK

PRINCE ALBERT N.P.

North Battleford

Prince Albert

Melfort

Rosetown

Saskatoon

Hudson Bay

Swan River

Moose Jaw

Melville

Yorkton

Regina

Weyburn

Estevan

Swift Current

CYPRESS HILLS INTERPROV. PARK

GRASSLANDS N.P.

NARROW HILLS PROV. PARK

SAND LAKES PROV. PARK

Reindeer Lake

Flin Flon

Lynn Lake

Thompson

NUMAYKOOS LAKE PROV. PARK

GRASS RIVER PROV. PARK

CLEARWATER PROV. PARK

DUCK MTN. PROV. PARK

PORCUPINE PROV. FOR.

MANITOBA

Grand Rapids

Lake Winnipeg

Lake Manitoba

Dauphin

RIDING MTN. N.P.

Portage la Prairie

Winnipeg

Brandon

SPRUCE WOODS PROV. PK.

WHITESHELL PROV. PARK

NOPIMING PROV. PK.

Kenora

LAKE OF THE WOODS

Red Lake

Pickle Lake

Cape Churchill

WAPUSK NATIONAL PARK

Cape Tatnam

CARIBOU RIVER PROV. PARK

Northern Indian Lake

UNITED STATES

Estevan

Minot

THEODORE ROOSEVELT N.P.

Bismarck

NORTH DAKOTA

Pierre

SOUTH DAKOTA

Rapid City

BADLANDS NAT'L PARK

Grand Forks

Fargo

Duluth

MINNESOTA

Minneapolis

St. Paul WISCO.

Rochester

Sioux Falls

Sioux City

IOWA

Madison

ILL.

Fort Frances

VOYAGEURS N.P.

QUETICO PROV. PARK

MOUNTAIN TIME ZONE

CENTRAL TIME ZONE

PACIFIC TIME ZONE

Pg. 2

8 9 10 11 12 13 14

EASTERN TIME ZONE
ATLANTIC TIME ZONE
GREENLAND TIME ZONE

GREENLAND (DENMARK)

ARCTIC CIRCLE

DEVON ISLAND
Lancaster Sound
Cape Liverpool
BYLOT ISLAND
Borden Peninsula
SIRMILIK N.P.
Mittimatalik (Pond Inlet)
BAFFIN BAY

BAFFIN ISLAND
AUYUITTUQ N.P.
Iglulik (Igloolik)
DAVIS STRAIT
Melville Peninsula
Pangnirtung
Godthab
Cumberland Sound

NUNAVUT
Foxe Basin
Fisher Strait
PRINCE CHARLES ISLAND
SOUTHAMPTON ISLAND
Foxe Peninsula
Cape Kendall
Cape Low
COATS ISLAND
Cape Southampton
MANSEL ISLAND
Foxe Channel
SALISBURY ISLAND
NOTTINGHAM ISLAND
Hall Peninsula
Iqaluit
Hudson Strait

Cape Chidley
LABRADOR SEA
ATLANTIC OCEAN

Ivujivik
PARC NAT. DES PINGUALUIT
Povungnituk
AKPATOK ISLAND
Hebron
NEWFOUNDLAND AND LABRADOR
Lac Nantais
Lac Klotz
Ungava Bay

OTTAWA ISLANDS
Kuujjuaq
Cape Harrison
Cartwright
Port Hope Simpson
Mary's Harbour
Res. Manicouagan
530
TORNGAT MOUNTAINS
Nastapoca
Lac à l'Eau Claire
Lac Bienville
St. Anthony
510
500
Happy Valley-Goose Bay
Blanc-Sablon
Michikamau Lake
Lake Melville
430
FOGO ISLAND
Cape Freels
Bonavista

HUDSON BAY
QUÉBEC
Lac Burton
Michikamau Lake
Labrador City
Atikonak Lake
NEWFOUNDLAND TIME ZONE
NEWFOUNDLAND
St. John's
230
210
Grand Bank

POLAR BEAR PROV. PARK
Cape Henrietta Maria
Lac Sakami
Chisasibi
Radisson
James Bay
Natashquan
GROS MORNE N.P.
Corner Brook
Grand Bank
ST. PIERRE AND MIQUELON (France)
GREENLAND T.Z.

ONTARIO
AKIMISKI ISLAND
CHARLTON I.
Waskaganish
RÉSERVE FAUNIQUE DES LACS-ALBANEL-MISTASSINI-ET-WACONICHI
Lac Mistassini
Havre-St-Pierre
Détroit de Jacques-Cartier
ÎLE ANTICOSTI
Gulf of St. Lawrence
SABLE ISLAND
CAPE BRETON ISLAND

Matagami
Chibougamau
109
113
RÉSERVE FAUNIQUE ASSINICA
Sept-Îles
389
RÉSERVE FAUNIQUE DE PORT-CARTIER-SEPT-ÎLES
132
Détroit d'Honguedo
PARC NAT. DE FORILLON
Prince Edward Island N.P.
Sydney

Hearst
11
Geraldton
Nipigon
Timmins
Rouyn-Noranda
Val-d'Or
167
St-Félicien
169
Saguenay
170
RÉSERVE FAUNIQUE ASHUAPMUSHUAN
Baie-Comeau
Rimouski
132
PARC NAT. DE LA GASPÉSIE
Campbellton
Bathurst
104
Charlottetown
P.E.I.

11 17
Thunder Bay
Wawa
101
66
Lake Nipigon
North Bay
155
La Mauricie N.P.
Edmundston
NEW BRUNSWICK
Moncton
11
104
NOVA SCOTIA
105
7

PUKASKWA N.P.
ISLE ROYALE N.P.
Keweenaw Point
Lake Superior
Sault Ste. Marie
Sudbury
Pembroke
RÉSERVE FAUNIQUE LA VÉRENDRYE
La Tuque
Mont-Laurier
Trois-Rivières
Québec
Drummondville
MAINE
Fredericton
Fundy N.P.
Saint John
95
KEJIMKUJIK N.P.
Halifax
103

WISCONSIN
Green Bay
MANITOULIN ISLAND
Killarney Prov. Pk.
69
Georgian Bay Is. N.P.
12
Gatineau
Ottawa
416
105
Cornwall
St. Lawrence Is. N.P.
VT
N.H.
Sherbrooke
201
Acadia N.P.
Bangor
1
Boy of Fundy
Augusta
ATLANTIC OCEAN
Cape Sable

Mackinaw City
23
Georgian Bay
Peterborough
401
Montreal
117
Montpelier
Concord
Portland
Cape Cod
31
MICHIGAN
21
Lake Huron
400
Oshawa
Kingston
Watertown
81
Albany
Boston

Milwaukee
131
127
Toronto
Hamilton
Rochester
Syracuse
APP AL
MASS.
Providence
R.I.

Mississauga
Kitchener
London
403
Niagara Falls
Buffalo
NEW YORK
90
Springfield
Hartford
CONN.

Chicago
Lansing
96
Windsor
Erie
79
PENN.
Scranton
N.J.
New York
94
75
Pt. Pelee N.P.
Lake Erie
Sarnia
402
401
80
16-1

© Rand McNally

0 100 200 mi
0 100 200 300 km

Ottawa inset:
0 1 2 mi
0 1 2 3 km
© Rand McNally
Templeton
Parc de la Gatineau
148
Gatineau
ÎLE KETTLE
Pointe-Gatineau
UPPER DUCK I.
Canada Aviation Mus.
105
Ch. Pink
Prom. de la Gatineau
Hull
Rideau Hall
Rockcliffe Park
34
Vanier
QUEENSWAY
174
148
Mus. can. de l'histoire
417
115
113
Royal Ottawa
Ch. d'Aylmer
Parliament Hill
Univ. of Ottawa
Industrial
Hippodrome d'Aylmer
QUÉ.
ONT.
Univ. du Québec
38
Carleton Univ.
Smyth Rd.
Canada Sci. & Tech. Mus.
Des-chênes
Scott St.
119
118
Place
124
Central Experimental Farm
Heron
Ottawa
Carling
Richmond Rd.
126
73
Mooneys Bay
31
Hunt Club
Blossom Park
QUEENSWAY
Lac Deschênes
417
Nepean
127
Baseline Rd.
Woodroffe Av.
Prince of Wales Dr.
CANADIAN FORCES BASE OTTAWA SOUTH
129
130
416
Algonquin Coll.
32
Ottawa Int'l Arpt.

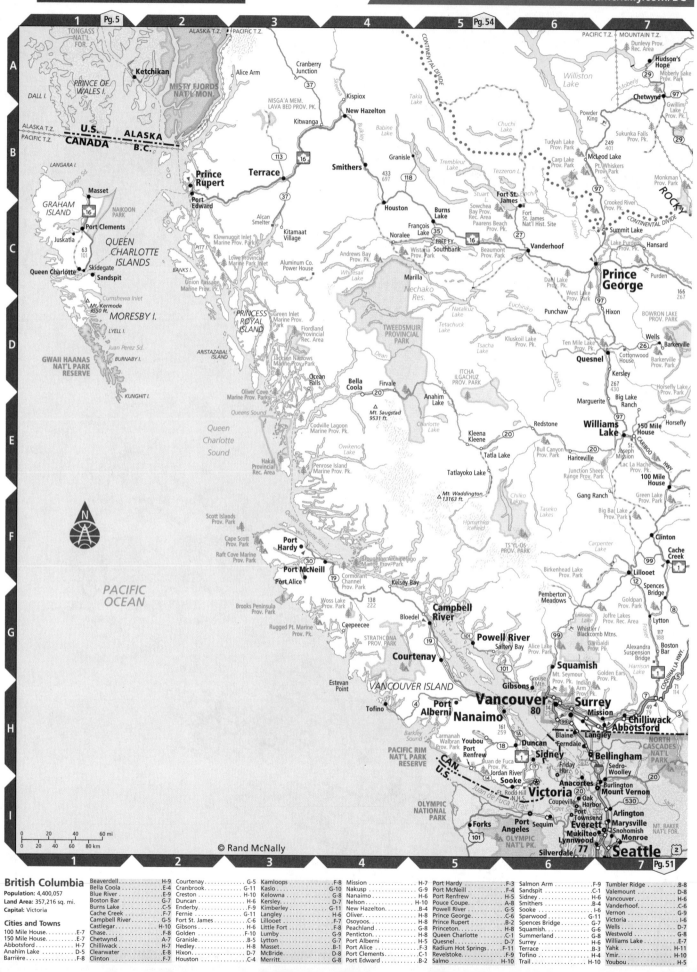

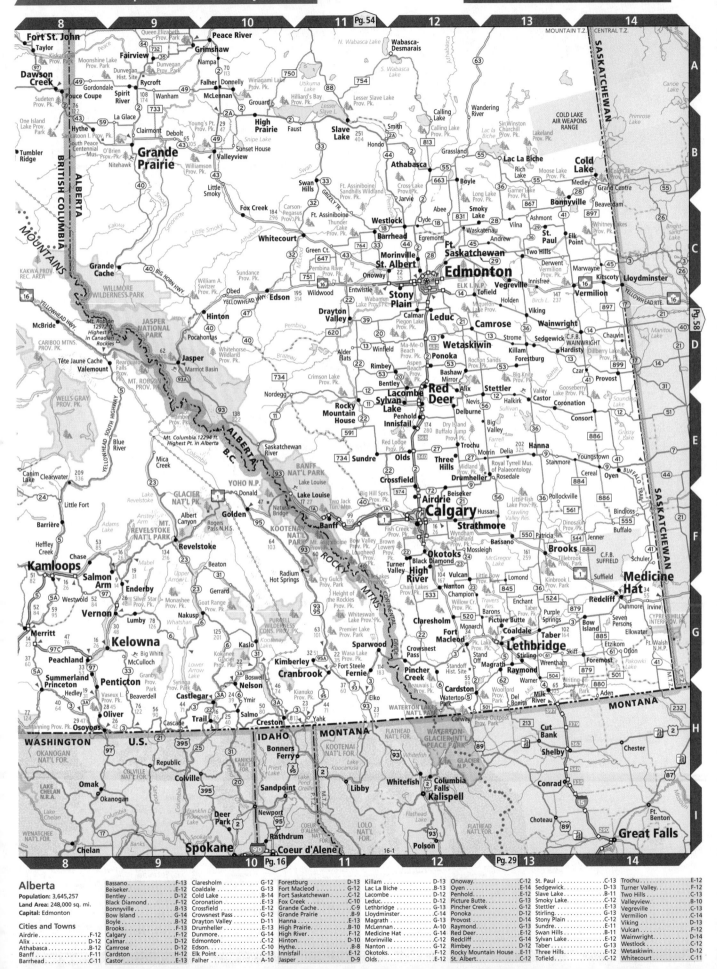

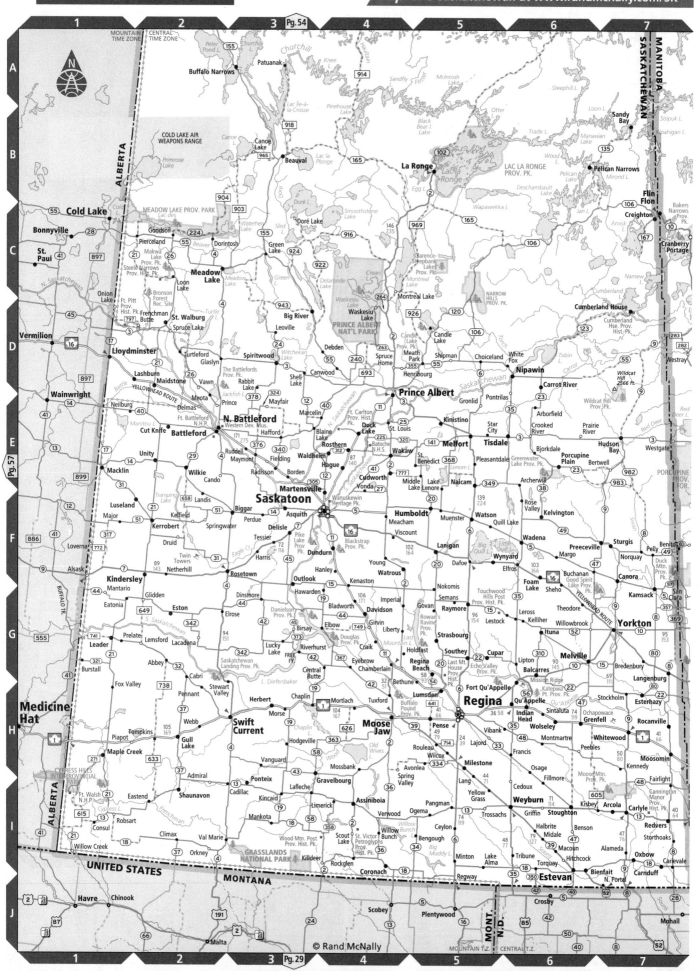

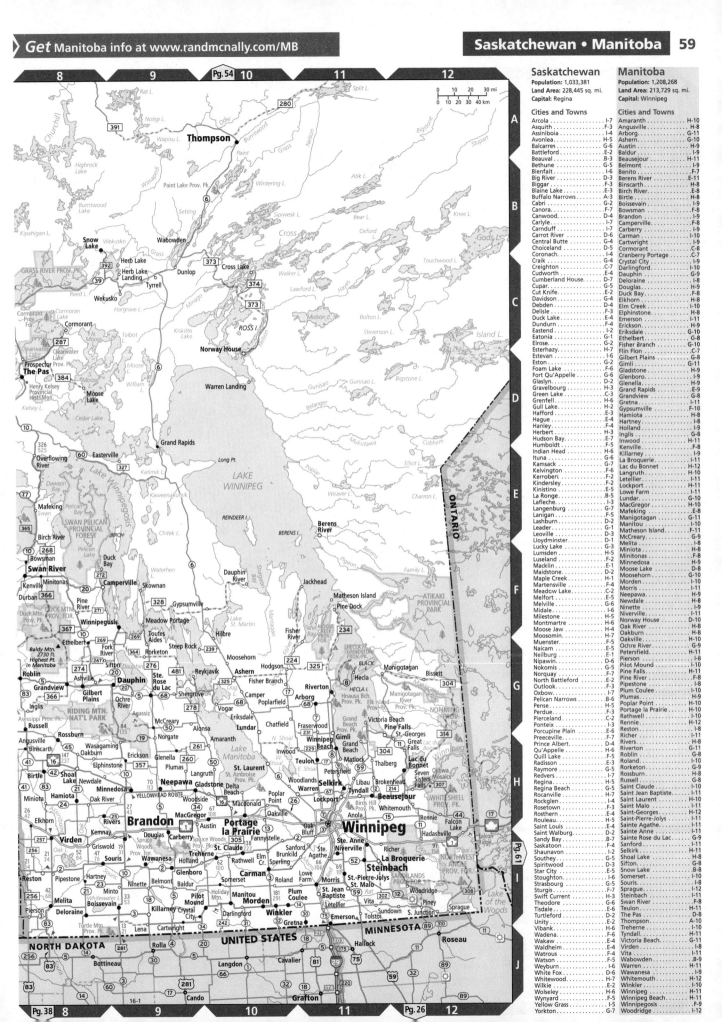

Saskatchewan
Population: 1,033,381
Land Area: 228,445 sq. mi.
Capital: Regina

Cities and Towns

Arcola	I-7
Asquith	F-3
Assiniboia	I-4
Avonlea	H-5
Balcarres	G-6
Battleford	E-2
Beauval	B-3
Bethune	G-5
Bienfait	I-6
Big River	D-3
Biggar	F-3
Blaine Lake	E-3
Buffalo Narrows	A-3
Cabri	G-2
Canora	F-7
Canwood	D-4
Carlyle	I-7
Carnduff	I-7
Carrot River	D-6
Central Butte	G-4
Choiceland	D-5
Coronach	I-4
Craik	G-4
Creighton	C-7
Cudworth	E-4
Cumberland House	D-7
Cupar	G-5
Cut Knife	E-2
Davidson	G-4
Debden	D-4
Delisle	F-3
Duck Lake	E-4
Dundurn	F-4
Eastend	I-2
Eatonia	G-1
Elrose	G-2
Esterhazy	H-7
Estevan	I-6
Eston	G-2
Foam Lake	F-6
Fort Qu'Appelle	G-6
Glaslyn	D-2
Gravelbourg	H-3
Green Lake	C-3
Grenfell	H-6
Gull Lake	H-2
Hafford	E-4
Hague	E-4
Hanley	F-4
Herbert	H-3
Hudson Bay	E-7
Humboldt	F-5
Indian Head	H-6
Ituna	G-6
Kamsack	G-7
Kelvington	F-6
Kerrobert	F-2
Kindersley	G-2
Kinistino	E-5
La Ronge	B-5
Lafleche	I-3
Langenburg	G-7
Lanigan	F-5
Lashburn	D-2
Leader	G-1
Leoville	D-3
Lloydminster	D-1
Lucky Lake	G-3
Lumsden	H-5
Luseland	F-2
Macklin	E-1
Maidstone	D-2
Maple Creek	H-1
Martensville	F-4
Meadow Lake	C-2
Melfort	E-5
Melville	G-6
Midale	H-6
Milestone	H-5
Montmartre	H-6
Moose Jaw	H-4
Moosomin	H-7
Muenster	F-5
Naicam	E-5
Neilburg	E-1
Nipawin	D-6
Nokomis	G-5
Norquay	F-7
North Battleford	E-2
Outlook	F-3
Oxbow	I-7
Pelican Narrows	B-6
Pense	H-5
Perdue	F-3
Pierceland	C-2
Ponteix	I-3
Porcupine Plain	E-6
Preeceville	F-7
Prince Albert	D-4
Qu'Appelle	H-5
Quill Lake	F-5
Radisson	E-3
Raymore	G-5
Redvers	I-7
Regina	H-5
Regina Beach	G-5
Rocanville	H-7
Rockglen	I-4
Rosetown	F-3
Rosthern	E-4
Rouleau	H-5
Saint Louis	E-4
Saint Walburg	D-2
Sandy Bay	B-7
Saskatoon	F-4
Shaunavon	I-2
Southey	G-5
Spiritwood	D-3
Star City	E-5
Stoughton	I-6
Strasbourg	G-5
Sturgis	F-7
Swift Current	H-3
Theodore	F-6
Tisdale	E-6
Turtleford	D-2
Unity	E-2
Vibank	H-6
Wadena	F-6
Wakaw	E-4
Waldheim	E-4
Watrous	F-5
Watson	F-5
Weyburn	I-6
White Fox	D-6
Whitewood	H-7
Wilkie	E-2
Wolseley	H-6
Wynyard	F-5
Yellow Grass	I-5
Yorkton	G-7

Manitoba
Population: 1,208,268
Land Area: 213,729 sq. mi.
Capital: Winnipeg

Cities and Towns

Amaranth	H-10
Angusville	G-11
Arborg	G-10
Ashern	G-10
Austin	H-9
Baldur	I-9
Beausejour	H-11
Belmont	I-9
Benito	F-7
Berens River	E-11
Binscarth	H-8
Birch River	E-8
Birtle	H-8
Boissevain	I-9
Bowsman	F-8
Brandon	I-9
Camperville	F-8
Carberry	I-9
Carman	I-10
Cartwright	I-9
Cormorant	C-8
Cranberry Portage	C-7
Crystal City	I-9
Darlingford	I-10
Dauphin	G-9
Deloraine	I-8
Douglas	I-9
Duck Bay	F-8
Elkhorn	H-8
Elm Creek	I-10
Elphinstone	H-8
Emerson	I-11
Erickson	H-9
Eriksdale	G-10
Ethelbert	G-8
Fisher Branch	G-10
Flin Flon	C-7
Gilbert Plains	G-8
Gimli	G-11
Gladstone	H-9
Glenboro	I-9
Glenella	H-9
Grand Rapids	E-9
Grandview	G-8
Gretna	I-11
Gypsumville	F-10
Hamiota	H-8
Hartney	I-8
Holland	I-9
Inglis	G-8
Inwood	H-11
Kenville	F-8
Killarney	I-9
La Broquerie	I-11
Lac du Bonnet	H-11
Langruth	H-10
Letellier	I-11
Lockport	H-11
Lowe Farm	I-11
Lundar	G-10
MacGregor	H-10
Mafeking	F-8
Manigotagan	G-11
Manitou	I-10
Matheson Island	F-11
McCreary	G-9
Melita	I-8
Miniota	H-8
Minitonas	F-8
Minnedosa	H-9
Moose Lake	D-8
Moosehorn	G-10
Morden	I-10
Morris	I-11
Neepawa	H-9
Newdale	H-8
Ninette	I-9
Niverville	I-11
Norway House	D-10
Oak River	H-8
Oakburn	H-8
Oakville	H-10
Ochre River	G-9
Petersfield	H-11
Pierson	I-8
Pilot Mound	I-9
Pine Falls	H-11
Pine River	G-8
Pipestone	I-8
Plum Coulee	I-10
Plumas	H-9
Poplar Point	H-10
Portage la Prairie	H-10
Rathwell	I-10
Rennie	H-12
Reston	I-8
Richer	I-11
Rivers	H-8
Riverton	G-11
Roblin	G-8
Roland	I-10
Rorketon	G-9
Rossburn	H-8
Russell	H-8
Saint Claude	I-10
Saint Jean Baptiste	I-11
Saint Laurent	H-10
Saint Malo	I-11
Saint-Georges	H-12
Saint-Pierre-Jolys	I-11
Sainte Agathe	I-11
Sainte Anne	I-11
Sainte Rose du Lac	G-9
Sanford	I-11
Selkirk	H-11
Shoal Lake	H-8
Sifton	G-8
Snow Lake	B-8
Somerset	I-9
Souris	I-8
Sprague	I-12
Steinbach	I-11
Swan River	F-8
Teulon	H-11
The Pas	D-8
Thompson	A-10
Treherne	I-10
Tyndall	H-11
Victoria Beach	G-11
Virden	I-8
Vita	I-11
Wabowden	B-9
Warren	H-11
Wawanesa	I-9
Whitemouth	H-12
Winkler	I-10
Winnipeg	H-11
Winnipeg Beach	H-11
Winnipegosis	F-9
Woodridge	I-12

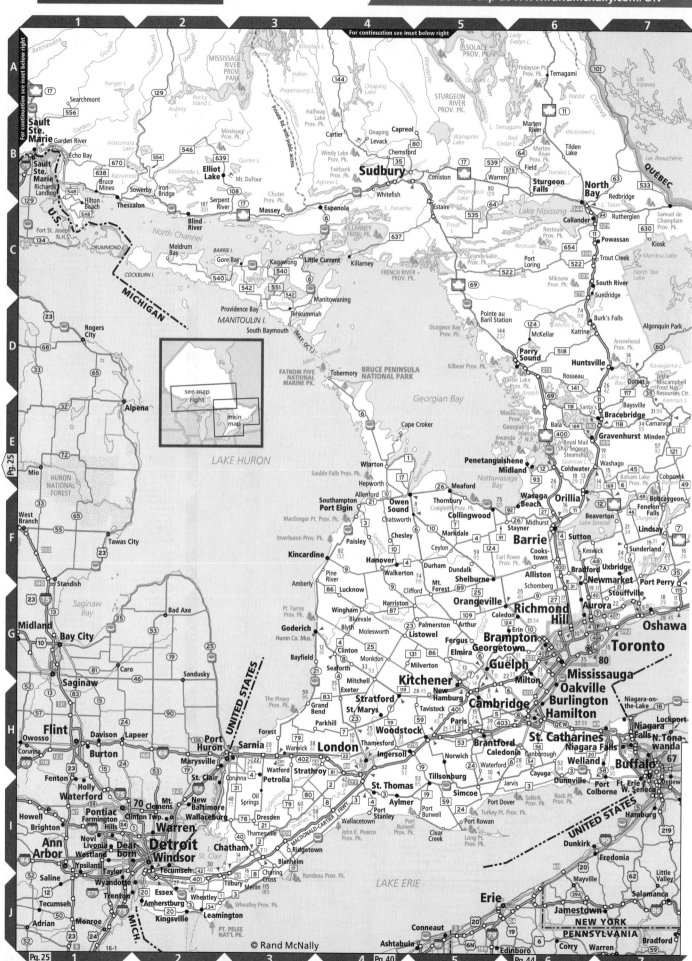

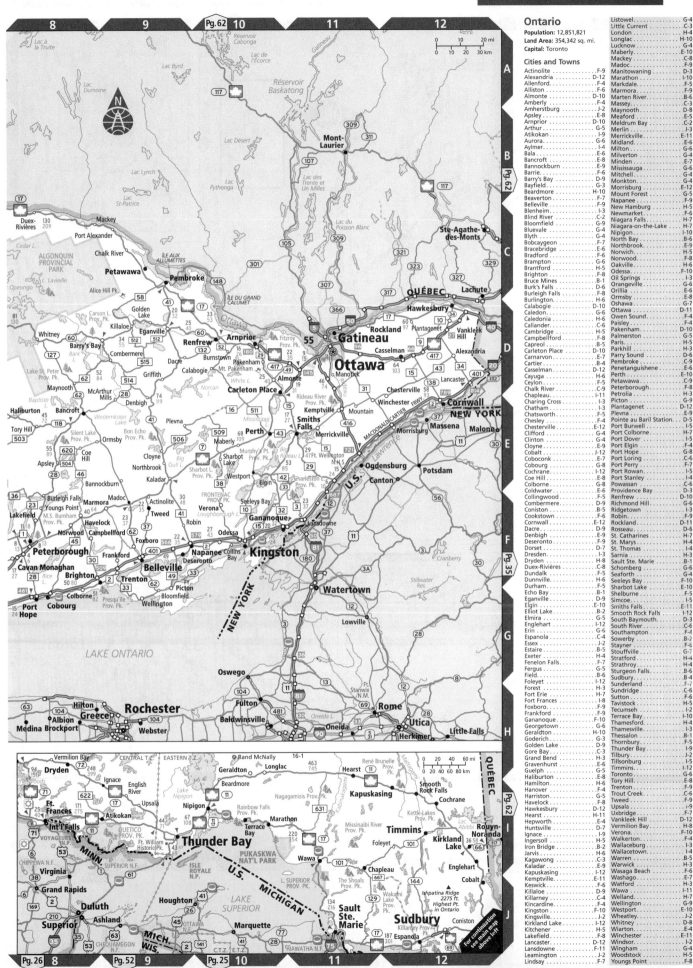

Ontario

Population: 12,851,821
Land Area: 354,342 sq. mi.
Capital: Toronto

Cities and Towns

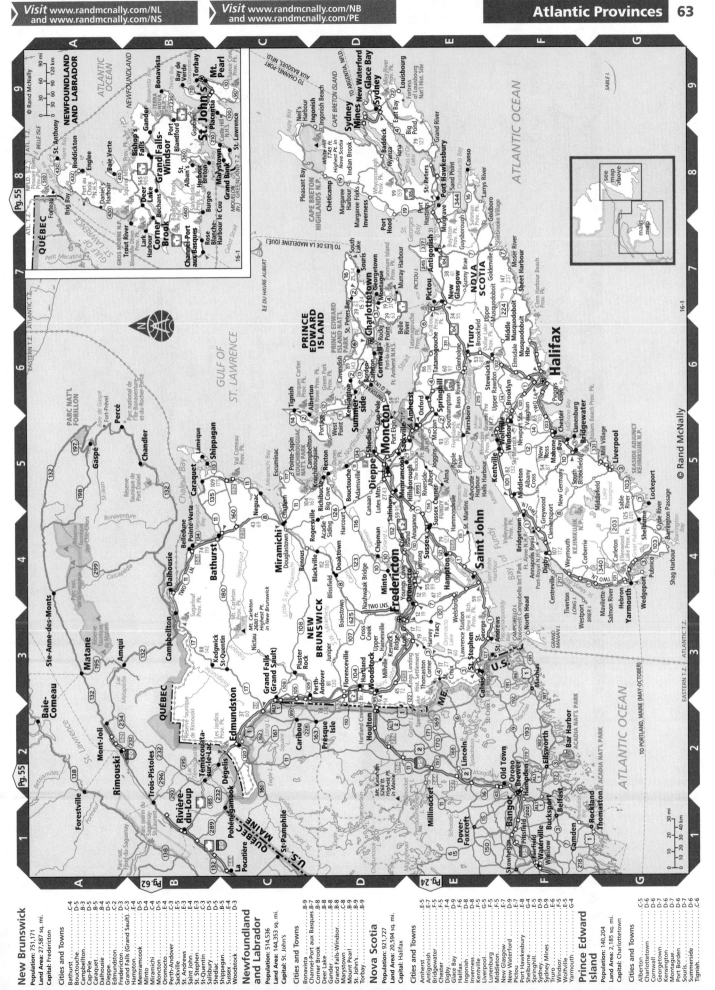

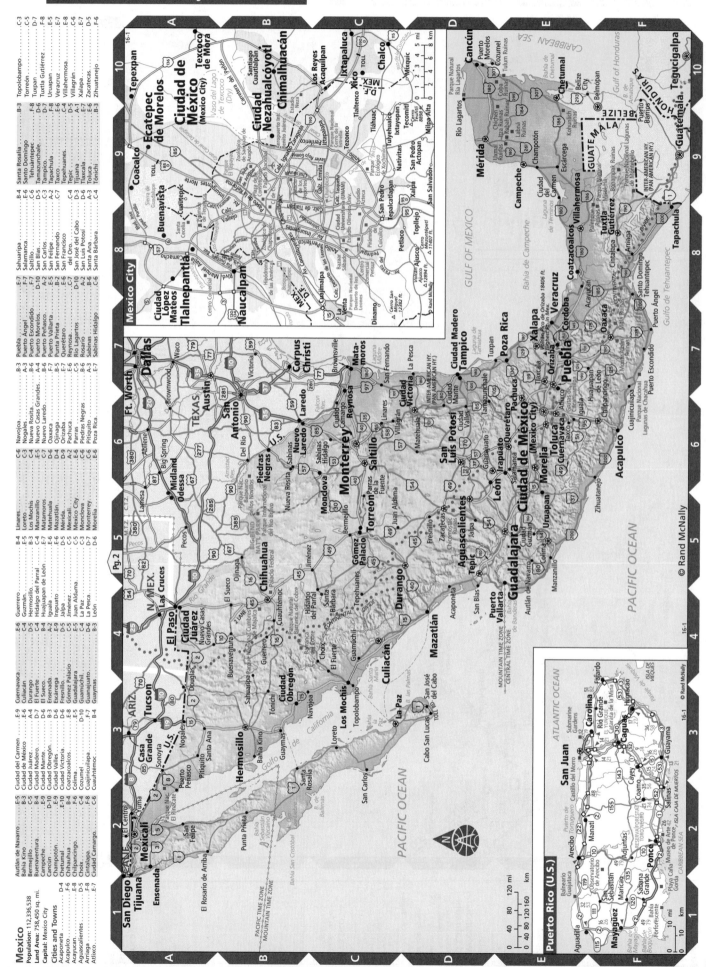

Mexico

Population: 112,336,538
Land Area: 758,450 sq. mi.
Capital: Mexico City

Cities and Towns

Mexico City

Puerto Rico (U.S.)

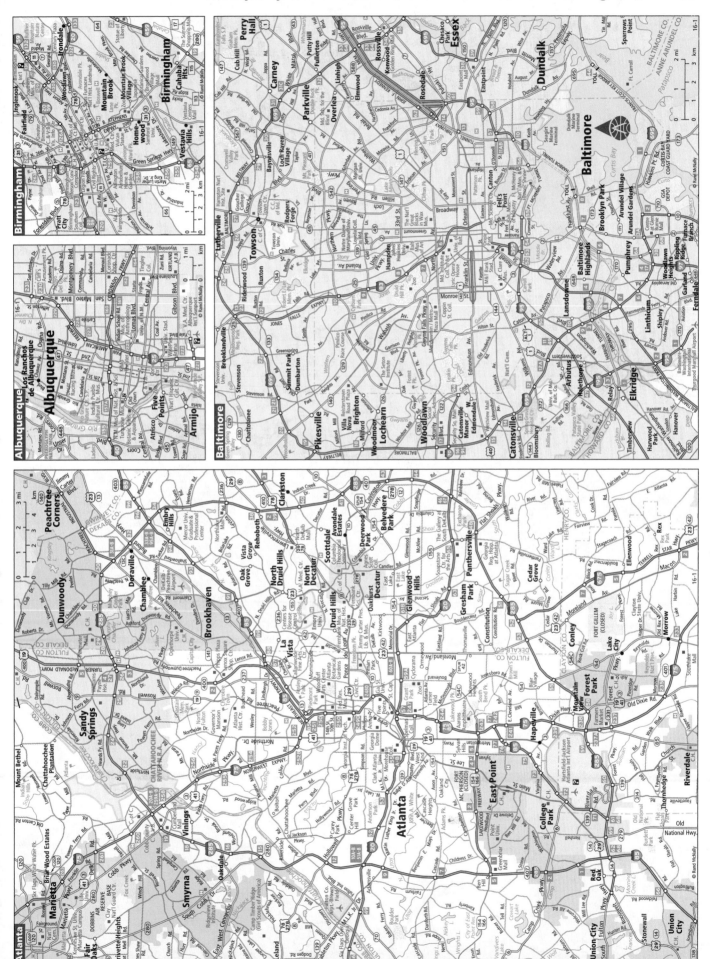

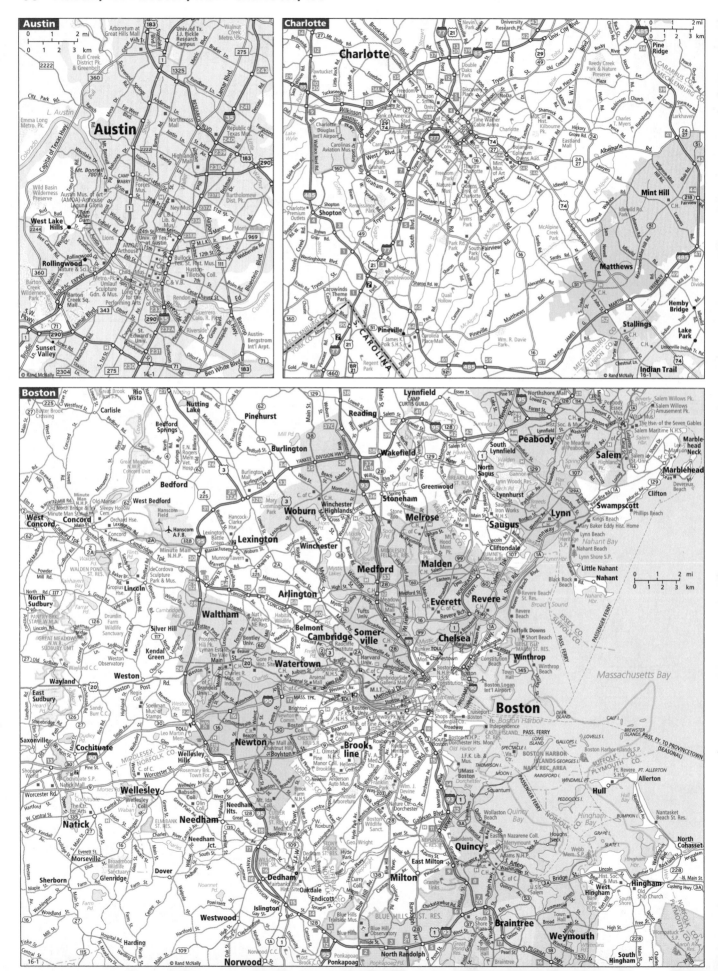

Chicago & Vicinity

Buffalo

LAKE MICHIGAN
El. 579 ft. above sea level

Chicago

Joliet

Naperville

Buffalo

LAKE ERIE

ONTARIO

Tonawanda
N. Tonawanda
Grand Island
Amherst
Kenmore
Snyder
West Seneca
Lackawanna
Blasdell
Woodlawn

Tower Lakes · Cary · Fox River Grove · North Barrington · Lake Barrington · Barrington · Barrington Hills · Inverness · Palatine · Arlington Heights · Rolling Meadows · Mount Prospect · Hoffman Estates · Schaumburg · Streamwood · Hanover Park · Bartlett · Roselle · Medinah · Bloomingdale · Itasca · Wood Dale · Bensenville · Carol Stream · Glendale Heights · Addison · West Chicago · Winfield · Wheaton · Glen Ellyn · Lombard · Villa Park · Elmhurst · Warrenville · Lisle · Downers Grove · Clarendon Hills · Hinsdale · Westmont · Naperville · Woodridge · Darien · Willowbrook · Burr Ridge · Bolingbrook · Romeoville · Plainfield · Lockport · Crest Hill · Shorewood · Rockdale · Homer Glen · Orland Park · Orland Hills · Tinley Park · New Lenox · Frankfort · Mokena

Lake Zurich · Long Grove · Deer Park · Kildeer · Buffalo Grove · Wheeling · Northbrook · Deerfield · Highland Park · Glencoe · Winnetka · Northfield · Glenview · Wilmette · Kenilworth · Evanston · Skokie · Morton Grove · Niles · Park Ridge · Des Plaines · Rosemont · Schiller Park · Norridge · Harwood Heights · Elk Grove Village · Franklin Park · River Grove · Elmwood Park · Melrose Park · Northlake · Berkeley · Bellwood · Maywood · Oak Park · Forest Park · River Forest · Cicero · Berwyn · Riverside · Brookfield · La Grange · La Grange Park · Western Springs · Countryside · Hodgkins · Summit · Bridgeview · Burbank · Hickory Hills · Palos Hills · Oak Lawn · Chicago Ridge · Worth · Alsip · Blue Island · Calumet Park · Riverdale · Dolton · Calumet City · Lansing · Harvey · Phoenix · Dixmoor · Posen · Robbins · Midlothian · Oak Forest · Crestwood · Palos Heights · Palos Park · Markham · Hazel Crest · Country Club Hills · Homewood · Flossmoor · Glenwood · Lynwood · Munster · Hammond · Whiting · East Chicago · Lake Forest · Highwood · Lincolnshire · Bannockburn · Riverwoods

ILLINOIS · INDIANA

© Rand McNally

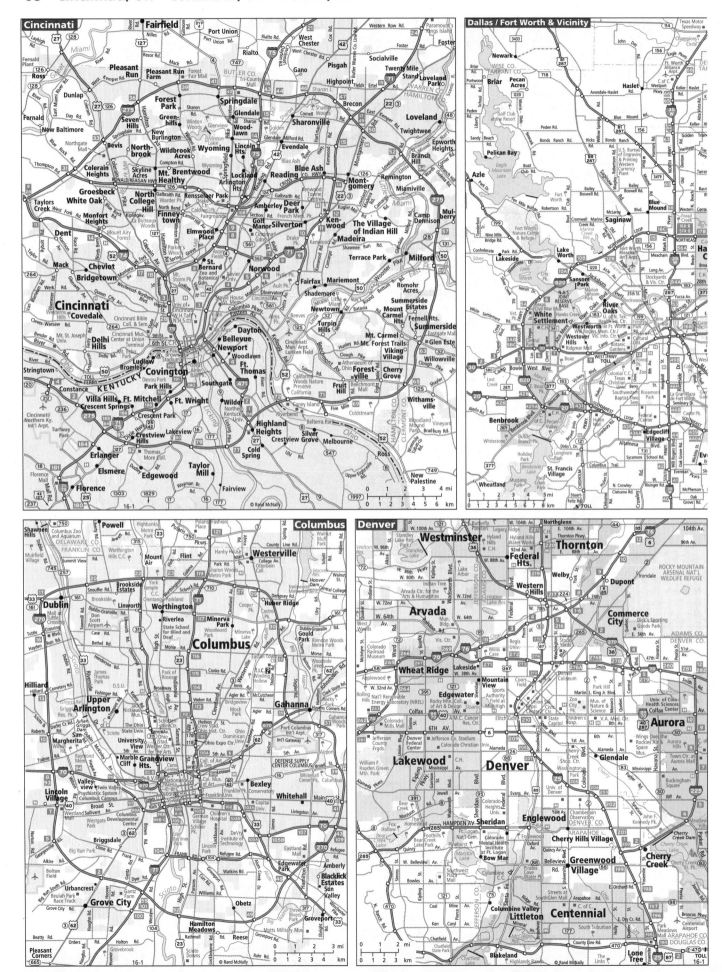

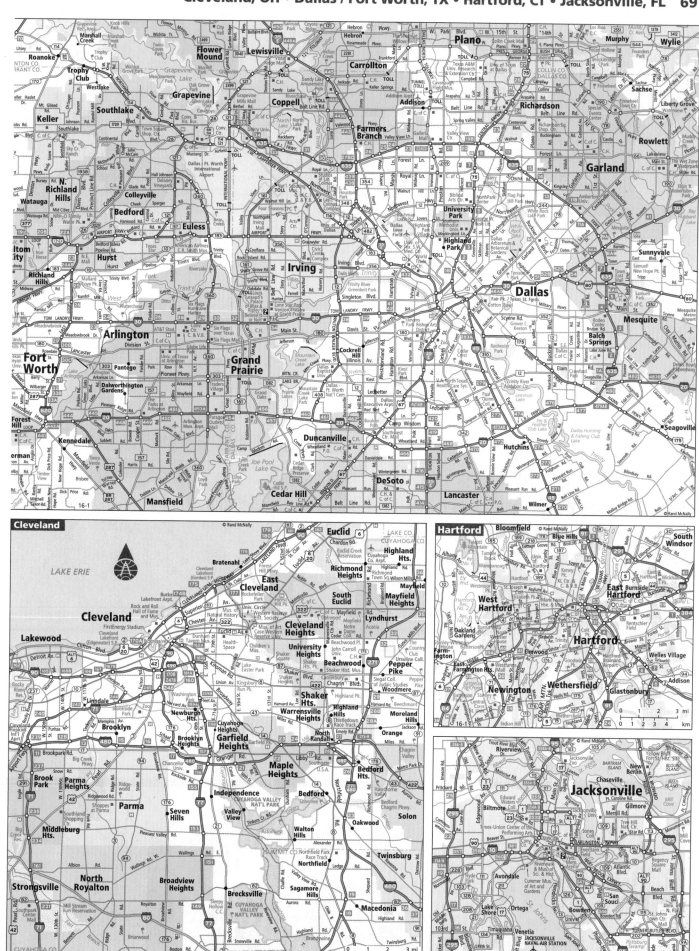

Cleveland

LAKE ERIE

Hartford

Jacksonville

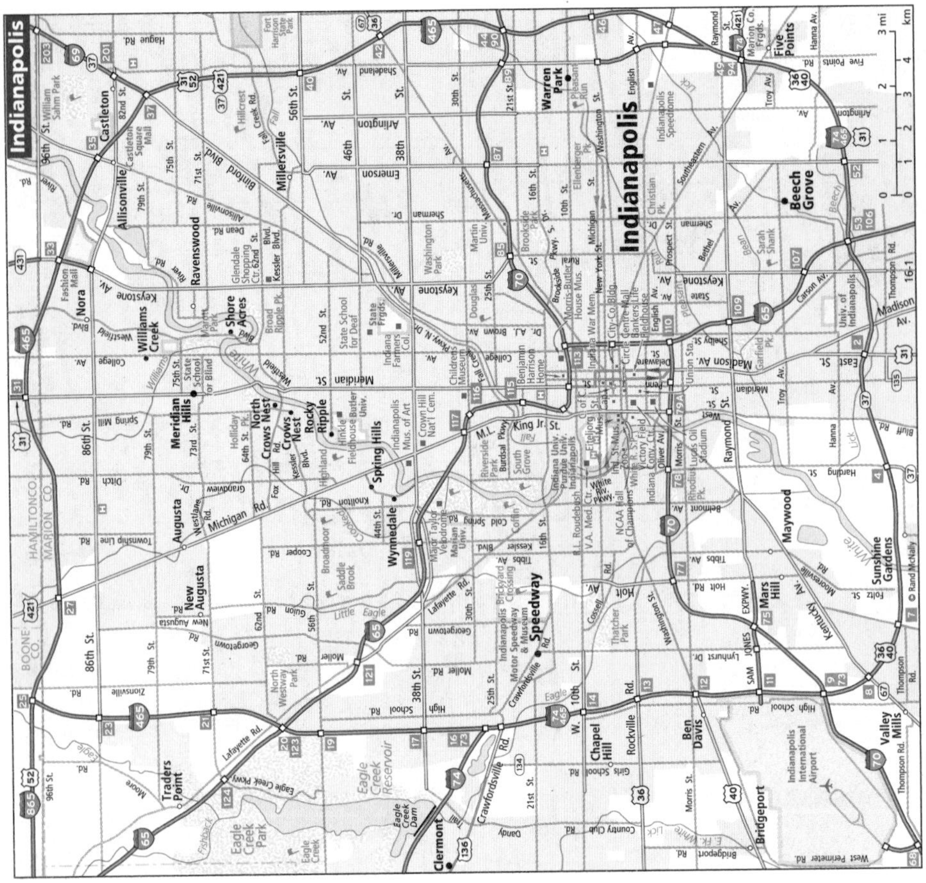

Indianapolis

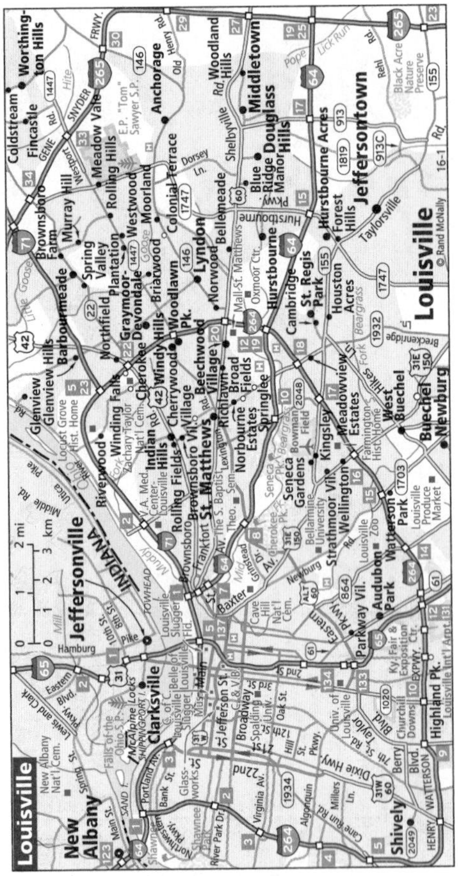

Louisville

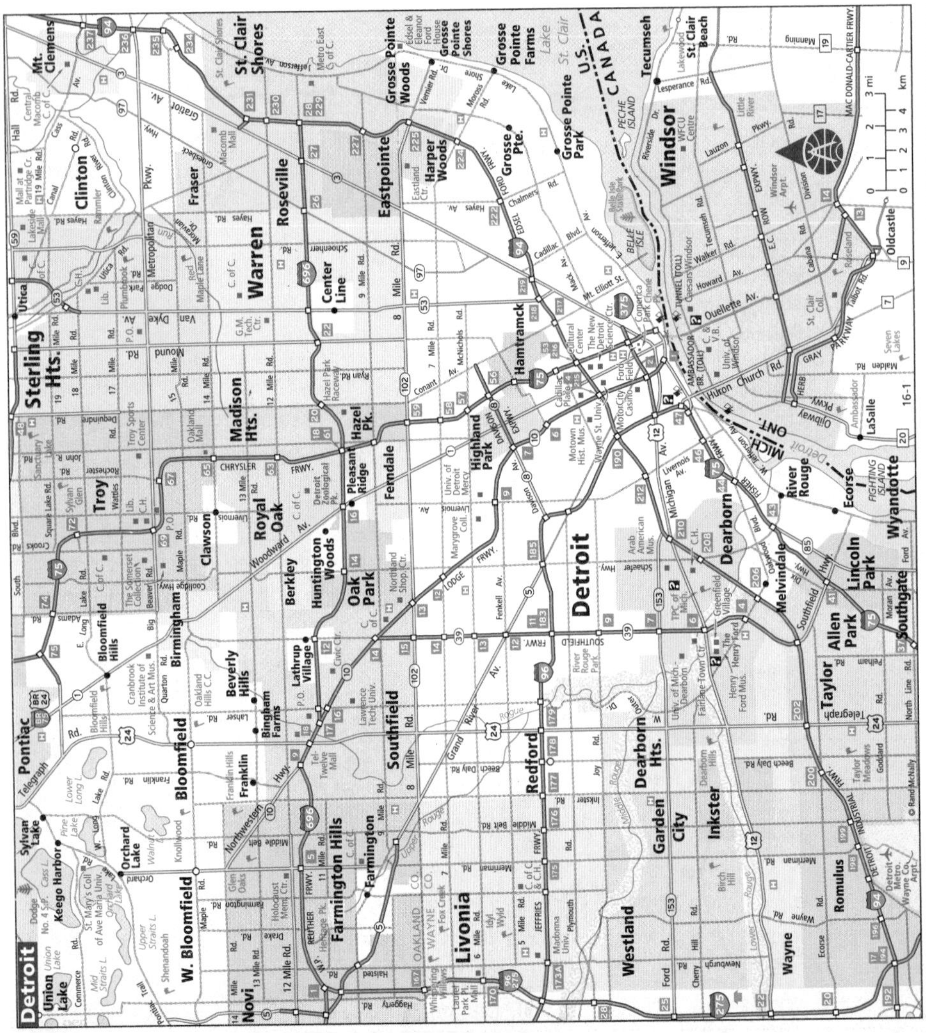

Detroit

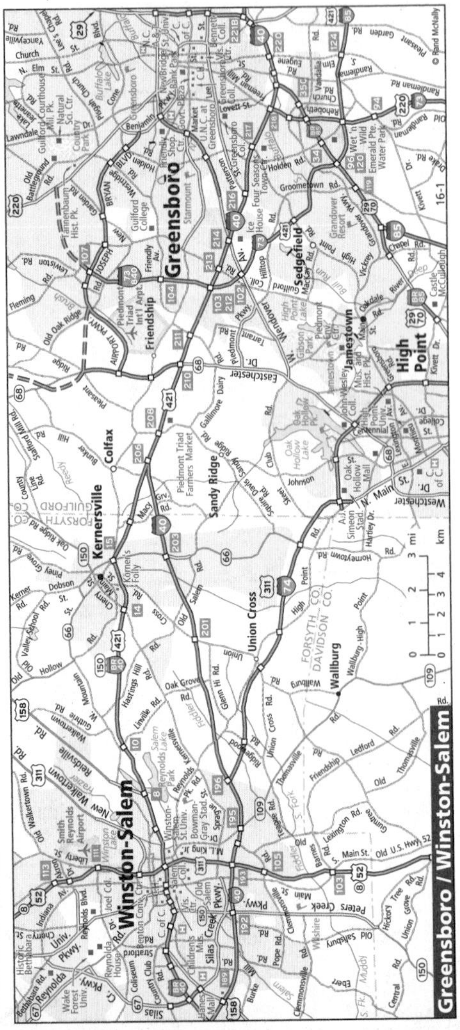

Greensboro / Winston-Salem

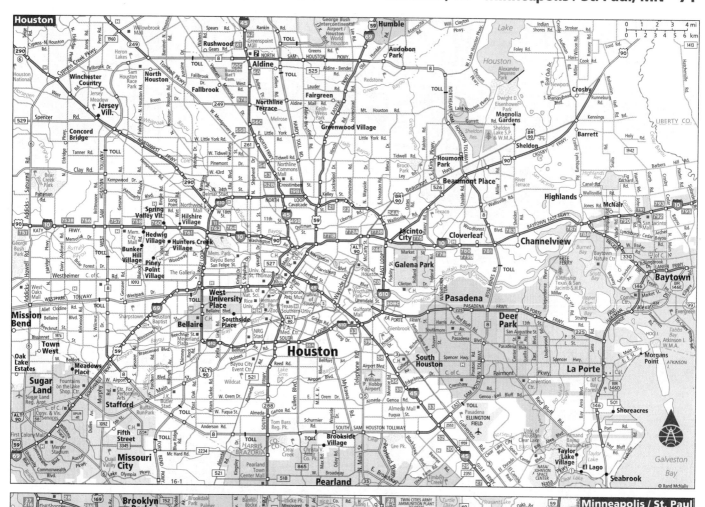

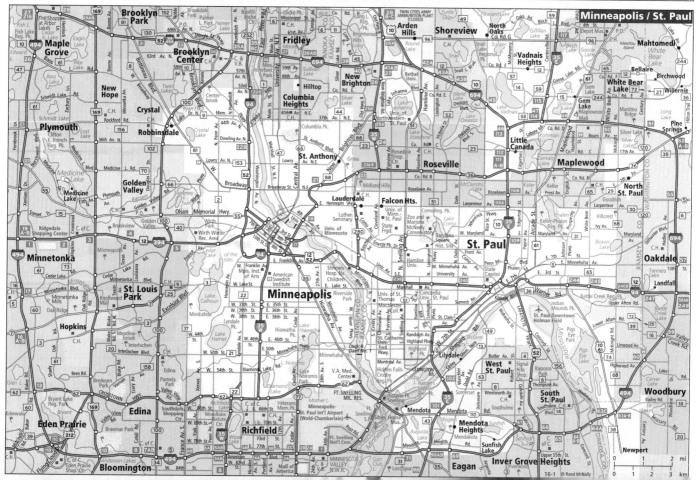

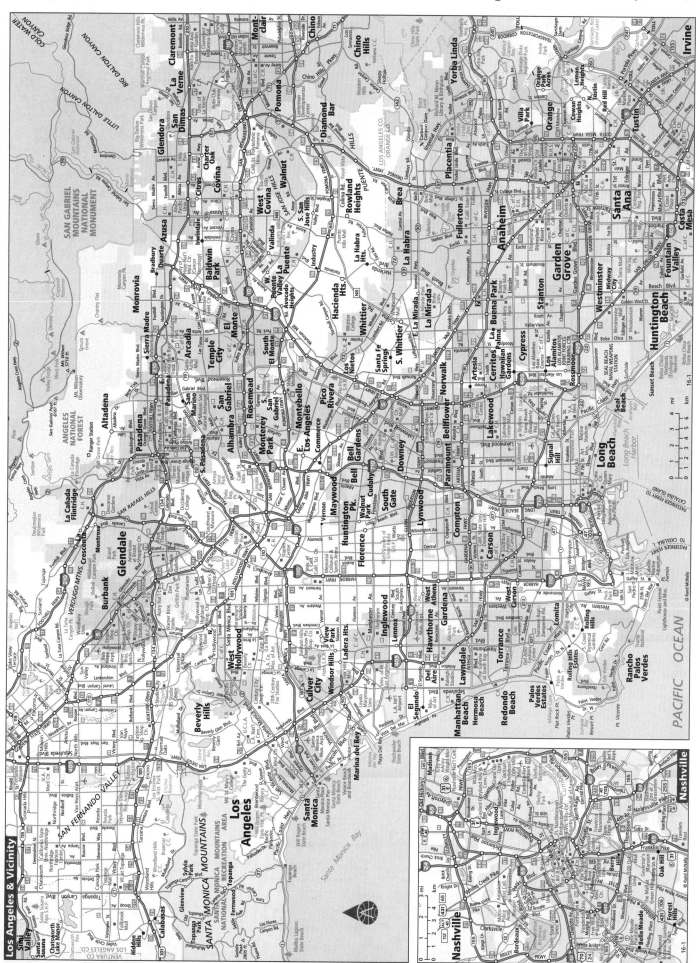

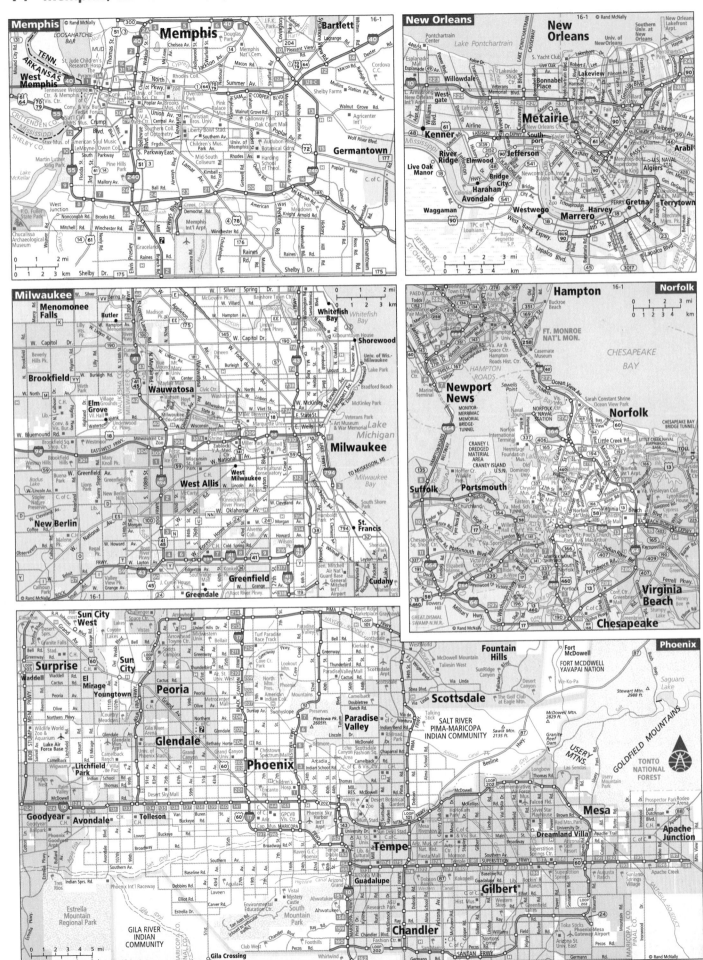

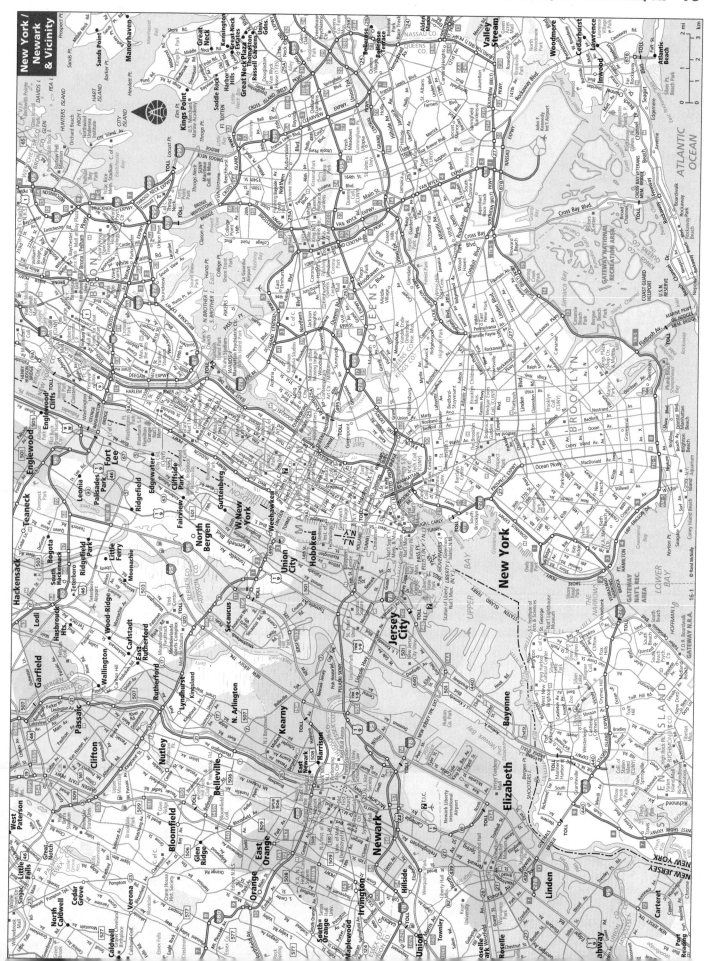

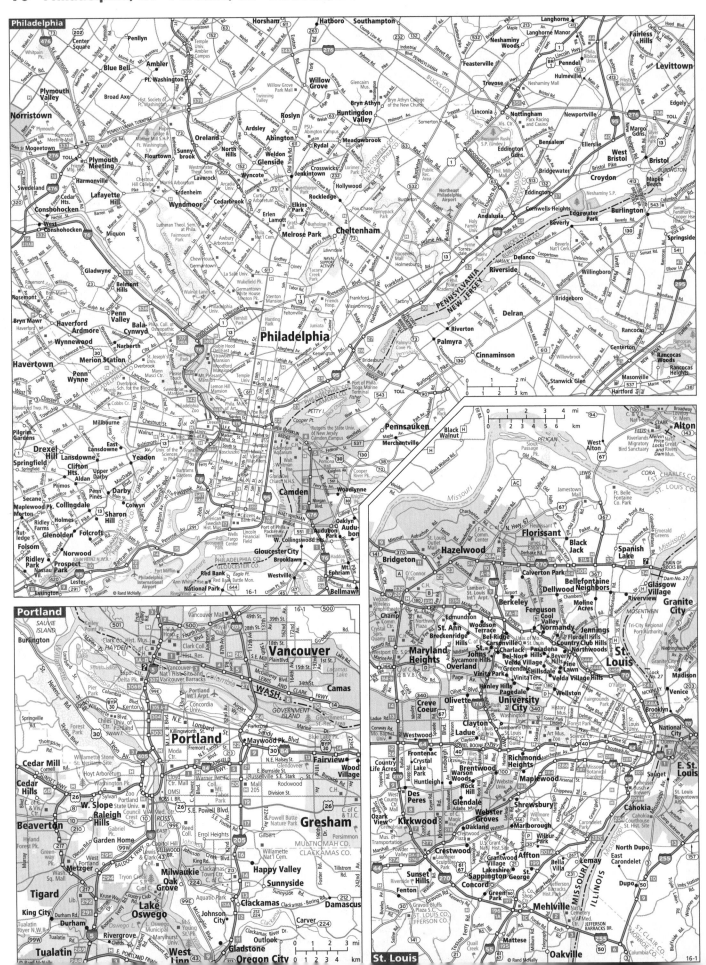

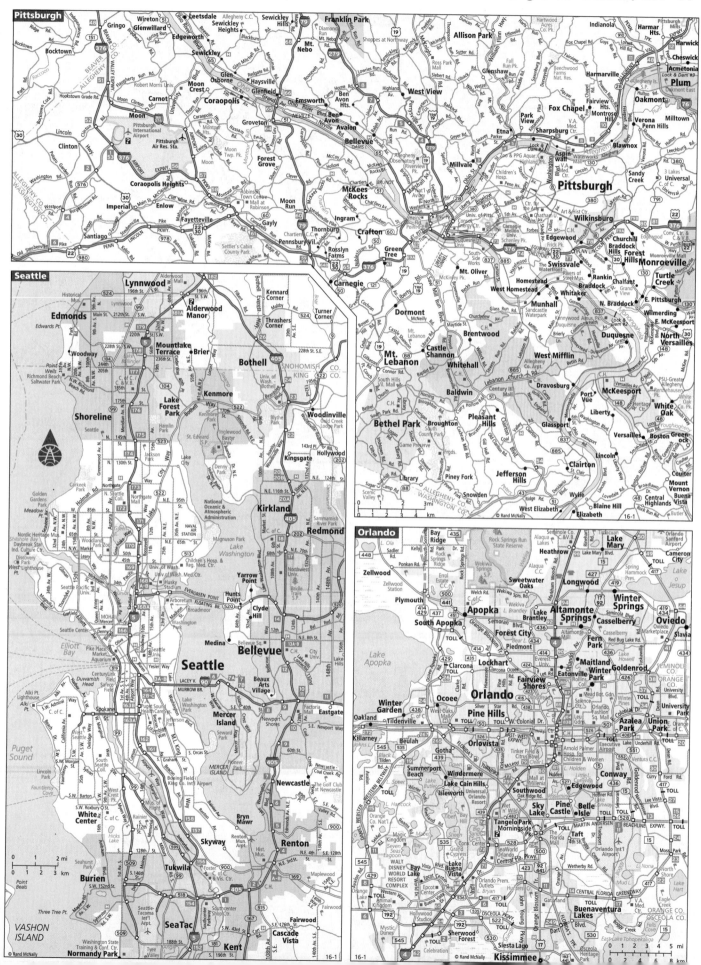

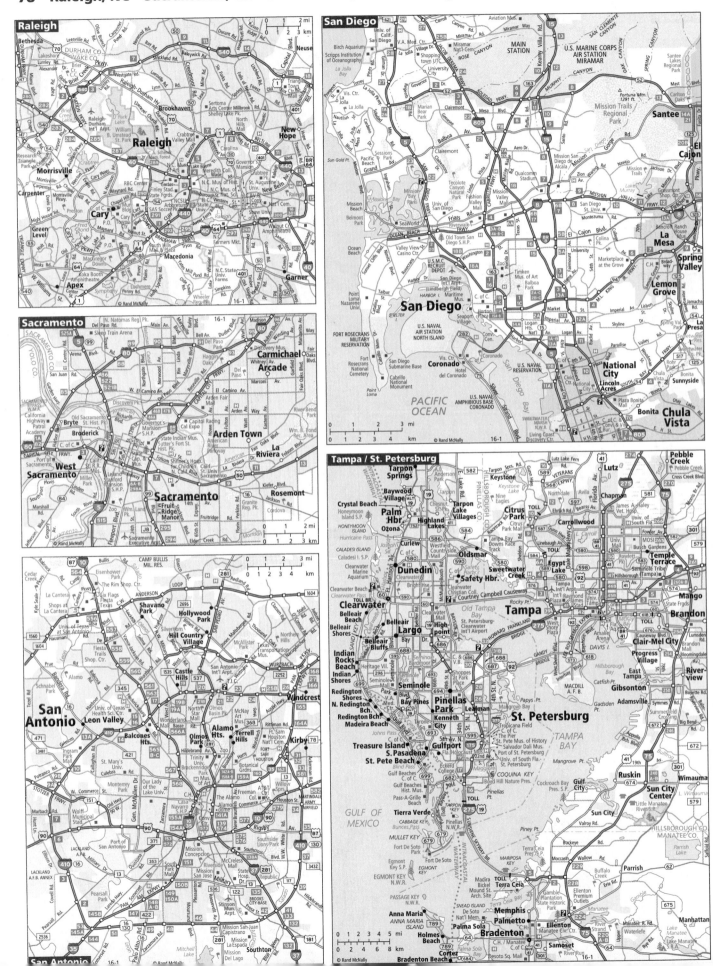

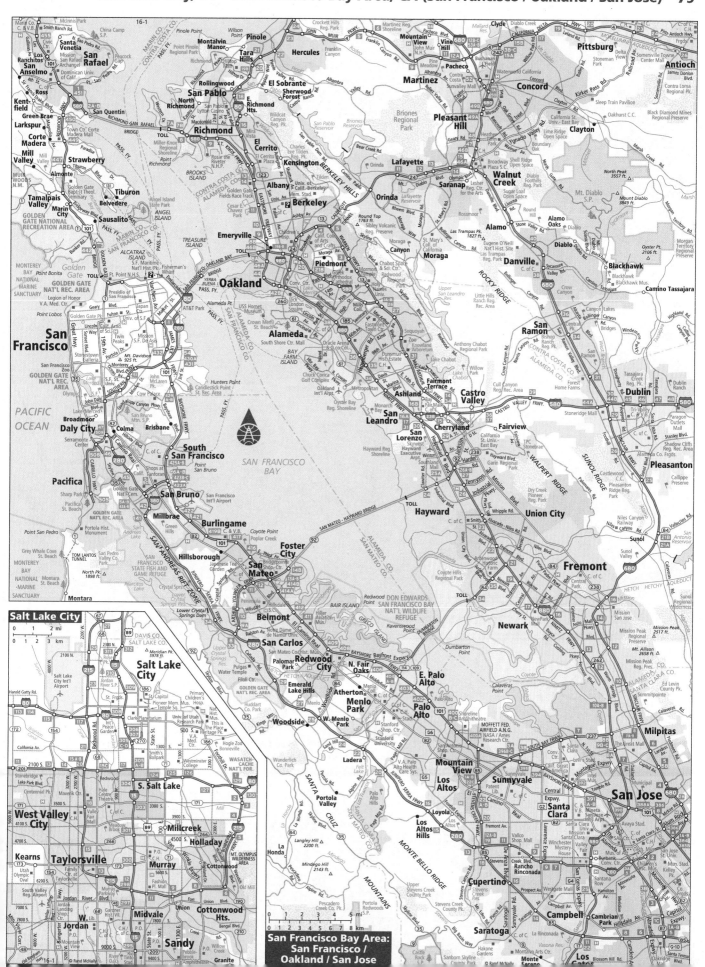

San Francisco Bay Area:
San Francisco /
Oakland / San Jose

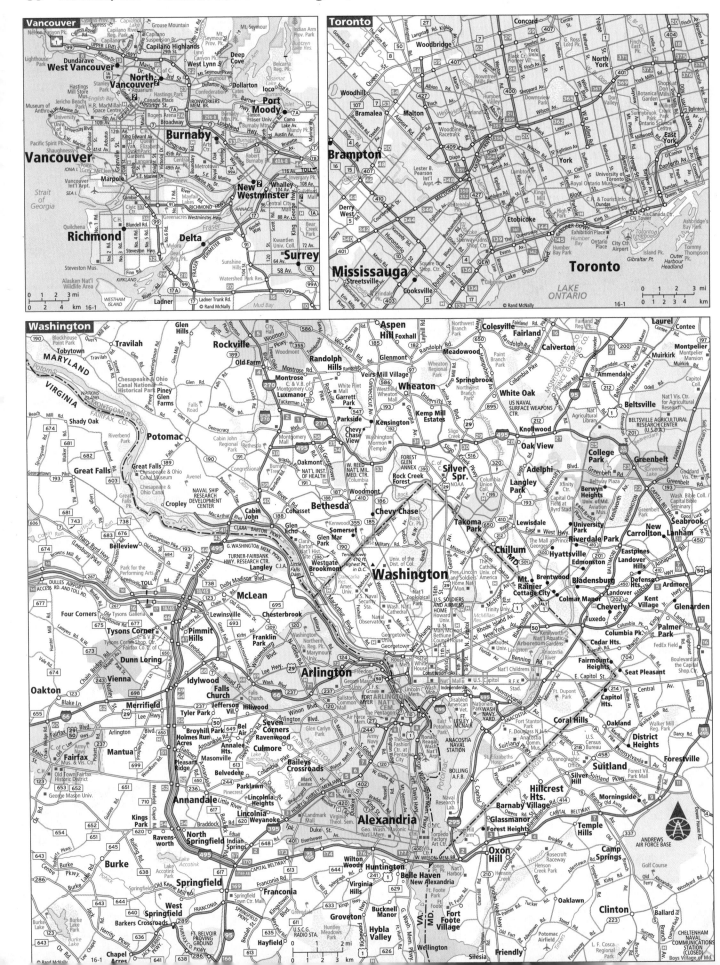

Hotel Resources

Adam's Mark Hotels & Resorts
(716) 845-5100
www.adamsmark.com

Aloft Hotels
(877) 462-5638
www.starwoodhotels.com

America's Best Inns & Suites
(800) 237-8466
americasbestinns.com

AmericInn
(800) 634-3444
www.americinn.com

Baymont Inn & Suites
(800) 337-0550
www.baymontinns.com

Best Western
(800) 780-7234
www.bestwestern.com

Budget Host
(800) 283-4678
www.budgethost.com

Clarion Hotels
(877) 424-6423
www.clarionhotel.com

Coast Hotels & Resorts
(800) 716-6199
coasthotels.com

Comfort Inn
(877) 424-6423
www.comfortinn.com

Comfort Suites
(877) 424-6423
www.comfortsuites.com

Courtyard by Marriott
(888) 236-2427
www.courtyard.com

Crowne Plaza Hotel & Resorts
(877) 227-6963
www.crowneplaza.com

Days Inn
(800) 225-3297
www.daysinn.com

Delta Hotels & Resorts
(888) 890-3222
www.deltahotels.com

Doubletree Hotels, Guest Suites, Resorts & Clubs
(800) 560-7753
doubletree3.hilton.com

Drury Hotels
(800) 378-7946
www.druryhotels.com

Econo Lodge
(877) 424-6423
www.econolodge.com

Embassy Suites Hotels
(800) 362-2779
embassysuites3.com

Extended Stay Hotels
(800) 804-3724
extendedstayamerica.com

Fairfield Inn & Suites
(888) 236-2427
fairfield.marriott.com

Fairmont Hotels & Resorts
(800) 257-7544
www.fairmont.com

Four Points by Sheraton
(800) 368-7764
www.fourpoints.com

Four Seasons
(800) 819-5053
www.fourseasons.com

Hampton Inn
(800) 445-8667
hamptoninn3.hilton.com

Hilton Hotels
(800) 445-8667
www.hilton.com

Holiday Inn Hotels & Resorts
(888) 465-4329
www.holidayinn.com

Homewood Suites
(800) 445-8667
homewoodsuites3.hilton.com

Howard Johnson
(800) 221-5801
www.hojo.com

Hyatt Hotels & Resorts
(888) 591-1234
www.hyatt.com

InterContinental Hotels & Resorts
(888) 424-6835
www.intercontinental.com

Jameson Inns
(800) 526-3766
www.jamesoninns.com

Knights Inn
(800) 477-0629
www.knightsinn.com

La Quinta Inns & Suites
(800) 753-3757
www.lq.com

Le Méridien Hotels & Resorts
(800) 543-4300
www.lemeridien.starwoodhotels.com

Loews Hotels
(800) 235-6397
www.loewshotels.com

MainStay Suites
(877) 424-6423
www.mainstaysuites.com

Marriott International
(888) 236-2427
www.marriott.com

Microtel Inns & Suites
(800) 337-0050
www.microtelinn.com

Motel 6
(800) 466-8356
www.motel6.com

Omni Hotels & Resorts
(800) 843-6664
www.omnihotels.com

Park Inn
(800) 670-7275
www.parkinn.com

Preferred Hotels & Resorts
(866) 990-9491
www.preferredhotels.com

Quality Inn & Suites
(877) 424-6423
www.qualityinn.com

Radisson
(800) 967-9033
www.radisson.com

Ramada Worldwide
(800) 854-9517
www.ramada.com

Red Lion Hotels
(800) 733-5466
www.redlion.com

Red Roof Inn
(800) 733-7663
www.redroof.com

Renaissance Hotels
(888) 236-2427
www.renaissancehotels.com

Residence Inn by Marriott
(888) 236-2427
www.residenceinn.com

The Ritz-Carlton
(800) 542-8680
www.ritzcarlton.com

Rodeway Inn
(877) 424-6423
www.rodewayinn.com

Sheraton Hotels & Resorts
(800) 325-3535
www.sheraton.com

Sleep Inn
(877) 424-6423
www.sleepinn.com

Super 8
(800) 454-3213
www.super8.com

Travelodge Hotels
(800) 525-4055
www.travelodge.com

Westin Hotels & Resorts
(800) 937-8461
www.westin.starwoodhotels.com

Wyndham Hotels & Resorts
(877) 999-3223
www.wyndham.com

NOTE: All toll-free reservation numbers are for the U.S. and Canada unless otherwise noted. These numbers were accurate at press time, but are subject to change.

Mileage Chart

This handy chart offers more than 2,400 mileages covering 77 North American cities. Want more mileages? Visit **randmcnally.com/MC** and type in any two cities or addresses.

City	Albuquerque, NM	Atlanta, GA	Billings, MT	Boston, MA	Charlotte, NC	Chicago, IL	Cincinnati, OH	Dallas, TX	Denver, CO	Detroit, MI	Houston, TX	Indianapolis, IN	Kansas City, MO	Los Angeles, CA	Memphis, TN	Miami, FL	Milwaukee, WI	Minneapolis, MN	New Orleans, LA	New York, NY	Omaha, NE	Orlando, FL	Philadelphia, PA	Phoenix, AZ	Pittsburgh, PA	Portland, OR	Saint Louis, MO	Salt Lake City, UT	San Francisco, CA	Seattle, WA	Washington, DC	Wichita, KS
Albuquerque, NM		1386	998	2219	1626	1333	1387	647	446	1570	884	1279	784	786	1008	1952	1354	1225	1165	2001	863	1730	1924	462	1641	1363	1037	599	1086	1438	1885	591
Amarillo, TX	284	1102	965	1935	1342	1049	1103	363	424	1286	589	995	570	1072	720	1668	1132	1009	881	1716	647	1446	1640	746	1357	1669	752	883	1370	1743	1600	382
Atlanta, GA	1386		1831	1095	244	715	461	780	1404	722	794	533	800	2174	379	661	809	1127	468	882	992	440	780	1844	684	2603	555	1878	2472	2649	637	955
Atlantic City, NJ	1985	831	2072	338	590	818	632	1518	1792	644	1598	703	1187	2774	1063	1248	910	1232	1273	126	1272	1038	60	2447	365	2922	948	2201	2934	2889	188	1379
Austin, TX	705	920	1495	1959	1164	1121	1128	193	950	1358	157	1067	702	1381	643	1341	1204	1136	503	1737	839	1124	1658	1010	1411	2068	825	1304	1760	2143	1524	542
Baltimore, MD	1887	683	1953	400	442	699	513	1368	1673	524	1448	584	1068	2670	914	1082	792	1112	1124	192	1153	889	98	2349	246	2804	829	2081	2816	2771	39	1260
Billings, MT	998	1831		2236	1990	1246	1546	1425	551	1535	1652	1435	1026	1240	1477	2497	1173	838	1868	2041	845	2275	2011	1210	1713	891	1278	552	1173	818	1951	1064
Birmingham, AL	1241	146	1780	1177	390	660	466	636	1329	724	668	478	749	2030	235	746	754	1072	343	960	939	534	880	1700	748	2551	502	1826	2327	2598	745	810
Boise, ID	938	2177	621	2660	2336	1693	1943	1702	830	1960	1930	1835	1372	842	1825	2844	1732	1461	2216	2465	1225	2622	2435	914	2137	428	1622	339	639	503	2375	1338
Boston, MA	2219	1095	2236		841	983	870	1764	1970	724	1844	937	1421	2983	1312	1482	1074	1396	1520	207	1436	1288	306	2681	570	3086	1182	2365	3098	3054	439	1613
Branson, MO	864	652	1241	1433	868	545	601	435	806	784	602	493	209	1651	274	1284	630	643	597	1201	402	1062	1138	1326	851	2013	249	1288	1950	2060	1081	292
Calgary, AB	1542	2357	541	2615	2400	1627	1925	1967	1925	1916	2209	1814	1567	1557	2028	3018	1555	1221	2419	2439	1387	2797	2391	1524	2093	1787	1820	869	1500	678	2334	1606
Charleston, SC	1703	317	2133	970	207	908	620	1099	1706	826	1105	726	1103	2491	696	583	1002	1324	742	768	1294	380	668	2165	654	2904	857	2180	2789	2951	532	1272
Charlotte, NC	1626	244	1990	841		769	477	1023	1566	616	1038	583	961	2414	619	728	867	1180	712	641	1151	526	539	2088	446	2761	714	2037	2712	2808	398	1092
Chicago, IL	1333	715	1246	983	769		289	926	1002	280	1085	181	526	2015	531	1381	90	408	923	787	470	1153	757	1795	459	2118	296	1398	2130	2063	697	724
Cincinnati, OH	1387	461	1546	870	477	289		934	1187	259	1055	108	584	2172	482	1127	381	703	804	637	722	905	571	1849	288	2369	348	1647	2380	2363	512	779
Cleveland, OH	1598	714	1597	638	514	342	248	1194	1330	168	1315	315	799	2342	729	1240	434	756	1057	460	797	1043	428	2060	131	2446	560	1725	2458	2414	370	992
Columbus, OH	1457	567	1606	763	426	354	106	1039	1261	191	1174	176	657	2244	587	1164	445	766	910	533	792	954	468	1920	184	2439	421	1718	2451	2425	411	851
Corpus Christi, TX	855	1001	1622	2051	1244	1338	1262	410	1077	1542	207	1228	919	1494	782	1191	1421	1353	554	1844	1056	1172	1754	1122	1561	2218	1042	1454	1873	2292	1619	758
Dallas, TX	647	780	1425	1764	1023	926	934		880	1163	228	873	489	1437	453	1307	1010	928	519	1548	636	1086	1467	1066	1221	2128	630	1403	1734	2193	1332	361
Denver, CO	446	1404	551	1970	1566	1002	1187	880		1270	1035	1083	603	1015	1097	2069	1042	913	1398	1775	534	1851	1732	908	1447	1256	854	533	1268	1320	1671	519
Des Moines, IA	983	902	946	1299	1057	332	580	683	670	599	938	474	193	1682	617	1567	371	242	1008	1105	137	1339	1074	1445	777	1786	354	1065	1798	1764	1015	391
Detroit, MI	1570	722	1535	724	616	280	259	1163	1270		1319	288	764	2281	742	1354	374	696	1066	613	736	1144	583	2032	285	2385	533	1664	2397	2353	522	964
Duluth, MN	1375	1187	860	1370	1239	466	760	1092	1063	754	1331	651	586	2076	963	1852	394	152	1354	1264	530	1632	1230	1838	932	1749	679	1458	2033	1677	1171	785
Edmonton, AB	1724	2391	722	2549	2443	1670	1968	2149	1278	1958	2391	1857	1626	1755	2147	3058	1598	1264	2538	2482	1445	2856	2434	1721	2136	966	1878	1069	1695	793	2377	1787
El Paso, TX	260	1418	1257	2373	1662	1455	1569	635	707	1702	744	1398	929	796	1089	1934	1497	1377	1095	2202	1004	1712	2102	424	1774	1630	1157	866	1175	1705	1967	730
Fargo, ND	1318	1361	607	1629	1414	641	937	1079	873	930	1321	825	600	1848	1054	2025	569	235	1445	1438	420	1807	1405	1780	1107	1497	841	1160	1781	1424	1348	685
Gatlinburg, TN	1439	196	1803	922	202	578	290	884	1376	552	964	396	773	2226	431	865	672	994	640	707	964	640	625	1901	493	2574	527	1850	2525	2621	490	905
Guadalajara, JA	1194	1739	2194	2789	1982	1954	1962	1028	1639	2191	948	1901	1535	1501	1482	2131	2037	1969	1292	2592	1672	1910	2492	1212	2261	2545	1658	1792	1963	2631	2356	1377
Gulfport, MS	1221	399	1912	1482	643	896	767	562	1386	1025	403	780	883	1949	365	792	1088	1416	78	1266	1073	572	1180	1577	1052	2633	647	1909	2307	2730	1036	867
Houston, TX	884	794	1652	1844	1038	1085	1055	228	1035	1319		1021	732	1550	575	1186	1163	1171	347	1632	898	965	1547	1178	1354	2356	784	1634	1929	2431	1411	595
Indianapolis, IN	1279	533	1435	937	583	181	108	873	1083	288	1021		482	2068	464	1198	272	591	818	707	613	968	643	1742	359	2260	243	1541	2273	2253	582	674
Jacksonville, FL	1636	346	2183	1146	379	1068	796	992	1756	1002	871	874	1152	2421	677	349	1163	1474	547	939	1344	141	844	2050	825	2954	907	2230	2723	3001	706	1272
Kansas City, MO	784	800	1026	1421	961	526	584	489	603	764	732	482		1616	451	1466	565	436	844	1196	187	1246	1127	1246	840	1797	250	1098	1851	1839	1066	193
Key West, FL	2099	809	2646	1659	886	1534	1275	1455	2252	1515	1334	1348	1617	2884	1159	162	1632	1944	1010	1446	1807	387	1357	2514	1332	3417	1370	2693	3186	3464	1213	1735
Las Vegas, NV	572	1959	973	2714	2199	1746	1932	1220	747	2013	1457	1828	1349	270	1581	2525	1786	1656	1739	2518	1278	2303	2480	286	2190	1023	1600	419	569	1128	2428	1164
Lexington, KY	1371	369	1610	917	400	370	83	876	1186	344	996	184	581	2158	423	1030	464	782	745	701	771	817	638	1833	370	2381	334	1657	2392	2428	533	773
Little Rock, AR	877	515	1407	1447	754	650	617	319	965	885	439	583	381	1666	137	1147	724	815	425	1230	574	925	1150	1340	905	2211	345	1488	1963	2275	1015	446
Los Angeles, CA	786	2174	1240	2983	2414	2015	2172	1437	1015	2281	1550	2068	1616		1794	2735	2055	1894	2387	2515	2713	370	2688	963	1821	688	380	1134	2670	1377		
Memphis, TN	1008	379	1477	1312	619	531	482	453	1097	742	575	464	451	1794		1012	622	831	394	1094	641	778	1014	1471	768	2245	283	1524	2095	2299	879	577
Mexico City, DF	1404	1718	2301	2768	1962	2017	1979	1090	1756	2254	924	1963	1598	1839	1500	2111	2100	2032	1272	2571	1735	1889	2471	1469	2279	2768	1721	2003	2218	2842	2336	1440
Miami, FL	1952	661	2497	1482	728	1381	1127	1307	2069	1354	1186	1198	1466	2735	1012		1475	1791	861	1288	1658	229	1180	2362	1173	3260	1221	2544	3038	3315	1044	1587
Milwaukee, WI	1354	809	1173	1074	867	90	381	1010	1042	374	1163	272	565	2055	622	1475		336	1015	879	509	1258	849	1811	551	2062	379	1437	2170	1990	788	763
Minneapolis, MN	1225	1127	838	1396	1180	408	703	928	913	696	1171	591	436	1851	831	1791	336		1223	1204	372	1573	1171	1687	874	1727	563	1308	2040	1655	1110	634
Mobile, AL	1234	328	1874	1427	571	917	721	589	1414	978	468	733	850	2014	382	719	1011	1224	144	1202	1038	497	1101	1643	1000	2661	645	1936	2320	2727	965	894
Montréal, QC	2129	1218	2099	310	980	847	824	1722	1832	560	1884	847	1330	2845	1314	1647	938	1262	1640	382	1302	1437	454	2591	603	2948	1092	2228	2960	2916	587	1529
Nashville, TN	1219	248	1586	1099	407	469	273	664	1158	534	786	287	555	2006	212	913	564	881	532	884	747	692	802	1682	560	2357	310	1633	2306	2404	667	688
New Orleans, LA	1165	468	1868	1520	712	923	804	519	1398	1066	347	818	844	1894	394	861	1015	1223		1304	1032	641	1222	1523	1090	2642	675	1922	2252	2716	1087	880
New York, NY	2001	882	2041	207	641	787	637	1548	1775	613	1632	707	1094	2787	1094	1288	879	1204	1304		1245	1089	97	2463	369	2891	954	2170	2902	2858	228	1391
Norfolk, VA	1910	558	2132	569	328	878	605	1350	1758	704	1362	720	1155	2707	898	950	969	1295	1026	370	1335	755	271	2373	425	2962	911	2238	2973	2949	189	1349
Oklahoma City, OK	542	844	1203	1678	1084	792	846	204	631	1029	437	739	348	1326	466	1876	788	722	1460	452	1254	1384	1005	1101	1922	496	1200	1627	1948	1344	158	
Omaha, NE	863	992	845	1436	1151	470	722	656	534	736	898	613	187	1546	641	1658	509	372	1032	1245		1436	1212	1325	914	1650	439	930	1662	1663	1151	298
Orlando, FL	1730	440	2275	1288	526	1153	905	1086	1851	1144	965	948	1245	2518	1573	641	1089	1436	986	2145	975		3048	999	2323	2816	3093	849	1365			
Ottawa, ON	2039	1158	1768	428	920	700	732	1632	1748	471	1804	757	1240	2763	1230	1618	859	1032	1582	440	1213	1408	447	2501	546	2660	1002	2142	2877	2586	566	1439
Philadelphia, PA	1924	780	2011	306	539	757	571	1467	1732	583	1547	643	1127	2713	1014	1180	849	1171	1222	97	1212	986		2387	304	2861	888	2140	2873	2828	137	1319
Phoenix, AZ	462	1844	1210	2681	2088	1795	1849	1066	908	2032	1178	1742	1246	370	1471	2362	1817	1687	1523	2463	1325	2145	2387		2104	1332	1499	653	749	1414	2348	1053
Pittsburgh, PA	1641	684	1713	570	446	459	288	1221	1447	285	1354	359	840	2428	768	1173	551	874	1090	369	914	975	304	2104		2563	604	1842	2574	2530	244	1035
Portland, ME	2315	1192	2333	110	938	1079	967	1861	2067	825	1940	1034	1585	3082	1408	1585	1176	1492	1616	304	1533	1385	402	2778	666	3186	1279	2461	3196	3151	535	1710
Portland, OR	1363	2603	891	3086	2761	2124	2369	2128	1256	2385	2356	2260	1797	963	2245	3260	2062	1727	2642	2891	1650	3048	2861	1332	2563		2050	765	635	172	2800	1764
Rapid City, SD	843	1508	323	1900	1670	912	1208	1061	397	1200	1291	1100	704	1312	1160	2173	840	575	1551	1675	525	1956	1675	1305	1378	1215	959	649	1384	1142	1618	699
Reno, NV	1019	2396	958	2881	2555	1913	2163	1668	1051	2180	1904	2056	1591	470	2029	3063	1953	1818	2186	2685	1445	2841	2656	733	2357	578	1844	518	217	720	2595	1558
Richmond, VA	1832	532	2010	547	293	797	512	1278	1671	622	1329	620	1002	2620	824	944	888	1210	1002	333	1289	742	245	2294	369	2869	822	2145	2880	2868	108	1261
Saint Louis, MO	1037	555	1278	1182	714	296	348	630	854	533	784	243	250	1821	283	1221	379	563	675	954	439	999	888	1499	604	2050		1326	2061	2096	827	442
Salt Lake City, UT	599	1878	552	2365	2037	1398	1647	1403	533	1664	1634	1541	1073	688	1524	2544	1437	1308	1920	2170	930	2323	2140	653	1842	765	1326		735	839	2079	1042
San Antonio, TX	712	986	1480	2039	1230	1202	1210	276	935	1439	197	1149	766	1357	727	1379	1285	1205	541	1822	920	1160	1742	985	1495	2076	906	1311	1736	2150	1607	625
San Diego, CA	810	2138	1302	3046	2381	2080	2196	1359	1077	2346	1472	2089	1597	120	1819	2656	2118	1986	1816	2809	1613	2436	2738	352	2452	1083	1845	750	501	1256	2693	1401
San Francisco, CA	1086	2472	1173	3098	2712	2130	2380	1734	1168	2397	1929	2273	1808	380	2095	3038	2170	2040	2252	2902	1662	2816	2873	749	2574	635	1801	735		807	2812	1775
Santa Fe, NM	58	1379	943	2212	1618	1313	1379	640	391	1562	877	1272	766	846	998	1944	1336	1207	1158	1994	891	1723	1917	520	1634	1388	1029	625	1144	1463	1879	572
Sault Ste. Marie, ON	1777	1040	1273	923	947	471	577	1370	1428	347	1527	540	951	2465	972	1685	398	538	1355	921	850	1475	911	2240	614	2166	740	1848	2581	2090	854	1150
Seattle, WA	1438	2649	818	3054	2808	2063	2363	2193	1320	2353	2431	2253	1844	1134	2299	3315	1990	1655	2716	2858	1663	3093	2828	1414	2530	172	2096	839	807		2768	1828
Spokane, WA	1320	2369	541	2774	2528	1785	2084	1964	1091	2075	2192	1973	1564	1216	2018	3035	1712	1377	2409	2580	1383	2814	2550	1381	2252	351	1817	720	878	278	2490	1600
Tampa, FL	1746	451	2316	1539	570	1166	912	1178	1860	1178	980	984	1252	2525	779	255	1260	1578	651	1138	1445	84	1040	2153	1023	3064	1008	2340	2832	3111	904	1381
Toronto, ON	1800	963	1771	548	756	519	493	1393	1504	232	1551	518	1001	2517	983	1483	609	933	1306	489	974	1284	497	2262	316	2620	763	1899	2632	2588	486	1188
Tulsa, OK	645	782	1234	1576	1022	687	738	258	692	927	487	635	243	1433	402	1414	773	704	671	1350	380	1192	1282	1107	994	1938	392	1215	1731	2012	1234	173
Vancouver, BC	1575	2785	953	3188	2944	2198	2499	2338	1465	2487	2565	2389	1980	1275	2437	3451	2125	1790	2851	2993	1799	3229	2963	1550	2665	313	2232	973	947	141	2903	1973
Washington, DC	1885	637	1951	439	398	697	512	1332	1671	522	1411	582	1066	2670	879	1044	788	1110	1087	228	1151	849	137	2348	244	2800	827	2079	2812	2768		1258
Wichita, KS	591	955	1064	1613	1092	724	779	361	519	964	595	674	193	1377	577	1587	763	634	880	1391	298	1365	1319	1053	1035	1764	442	1042	1775	1828	1258	

Mileages in this chart are based upon the routes usually followed by motorists. Highway systems include interstate, U.S., and state highways.

Mileages ©RM Acquisition, LLC d/b/a Rand McNally